EMERGE
with SELF-LOVE

PAULA ECHEVERRI
ALONG WITH 11 INSPIRING WOMEN AUTHORS

ISBN: 978-1-960136-42-8

Table of Contents

INTRODUCTION

In a world where self-doubt and insecurity often stay in the shadows of our minds, there emerges a powerful collection of narratives that illuminate the path to self-love. *Emerge with Self-Love* is a tribute to the resilience and wisdom of extraordinary women writers who have fearlessly embarked on the journey of self-discovery and acceptance. Within the pages of this book, you will find a captivating collection of personal stories, each written by a remarkable woman who has not only conquered her own inner demons but also emerged as a beacon of self-love and empowerment.

It has been a long journey of discovery and learning for me since I wrote my first book, *Emerge,* and two other books as a co-author. If you are reading this, maybe you are also interested in learning about self-love as many people (mostly our youth) don't know how to develop and work nowadays. Unfortunately, because of social media and its unreachable standards, this is something that we should speak more about and cultivate every day.

In this book I decided to bring some powerful women co-authors with one thread in common: how they used self-love and kindness in their journey, peeling the layers to connect with the core of their hearts and souls. This is a book about life and stories of adversity and joy.

Some of these stories have a mixture of real, raw experiences that many women will say, "Oh, I know that." But others will say, "I can be like her or do what she did too."

Their journey will inspire everyone to overcome challenges of self-worth and transform themselves into something beautiful and unique. These authors, hailing from diverse backgrounds and experiences, invite you to explore the intricate web of their lives, shedding light on their transformative moments, challenges, and triumphant victories. Through their words, you will embark on a poignant expedition into the depths of the human spirit as they share their insights, lessons, and revelations on the profound concept of self-love.

My goal since I wrote my first book has been to give women, or anyone who faces a challenge, a new take on how to overcome their struggles with tools they were previously unaware of. I personally believe that people learn and connect through others' experiences. Another goal is to showcase these women's journeys and to amplify their voices to the world.

As you immerse yourself in the pages of *Emerge with Self-Love*, you will witness the transformative power of self-compassion, resilience, and self-acceptance. These narratives will inspire and empower you to embark on your own journey toward self-love, reminding you that no matter how challenging life may be, the capacity to embrace oneself is a radiant light that can guide you through even the darkest of times. Join us on this compelling literary voyage as these remarkable women writers reveal the secrets to finding self-love in their own lives and, in doing so, offer a guiding light for all who seek to emerge with self-love.

I hope you get inspired!

Paula Echeverri
3x Bestselling Author and Neuroscience Expert
www.neuromomceo.com

As part of this book, I was very proud to invite my mom to be part of this project. Why? Because of her, I know what self-love is. The impact of a mom on a little girl is huge. My mom and the other women around me had a huge effect on me in my early years.

I saw dedication, strength, and love for me and my family. My mom was the one who took care of people when nobody else did. She did this with her mom and my grandma, and many won't understand the problems she faced doing this. Only, my dad, sister, and I saw her struggling and how it affected her later in life because she faced abuse in her life at an early age.

I learned from her that LOVE is the answer but SELF-LOVE is the key, just like I named my chapter in this book, because thanks to her I learned that to love others you need to start with yourself first, as you cannot pour from an empty cup. Filling our own cup is key.

Here is her story.

RETROSPECTION IS A WAY TO UNCOVER SELF-LOVE

By Gloria Llano de Echeverri

Self-esteem is the way one sees oneself. It is a feeling of confidence and personal value.

Having good self-esteem is very important for general well-being and also for personal development. This work is done by each person with the experiences received in the first stages of life.

That is why you have to have a positive and encouraging attitude towards yourself; you must be aware of your strengths and weaknesses as well as achievements and mistakes. This helped me accept myself and perceive myself realistically.

The painful circumstances that I have had to live throughout my life helped me accept my mistakes and learn from them, giving me a lot of strength to move forward.

To build confidence, I had to practice internal communication, which meant talking to myself in a positive and encouraging tone. All of this helped me avoid self-punishment and negative thoughts. It also helped me have better self-esteem by surrounding myself with positive people who would encourage me as a valuable person in the society I lived in.

Well, as time went by, I did a process that required awareness, dedication, and optimism. I learned to have an appreciation of my person that was influenced mainly by the way I saw myself, what I am and do, my beliefs, and even my weaknesses to strengthen myself internally to continue facing life with a lot of encouragement and optimism.

It is confirmed that low self-esteem can affect our personal, professional, and social lives, which is why we must develop our strengths and values about ourselves as early as possible.

We must try to remember our achievements and appreciate our strengths, recognize the gifts and abilities we possess, and celebrate the small steps we take toward our goals.

During my time at school, I never had friends. This is because I was very distrustful of all the people around me. Harassment and humiliation from classmates and family hurt me a lot, lowered my spirits, and affected my self-esteem a lot as strong words leave a big mark on the heart and become a part of what you think and how you feel about yourself.

Luckily, things didn't have to stay that way; it seems that an inner voice plays a very important role in how you feel internally. When you think things like "I'm a failure," "I always lose," or "I'll never make friends," they affect you internally. I meditated and told myself "I'm going to think in a different way." This time I won. Next time I thought maybe I could have some friends. This inner voice is much more hopeful. And it helped me move forward by getting out of that tunnel I was in.

Many times I asked myself these questions: Am I too critical? Am I too hard on myself? The answer is NO. I am worth a lot as a person. I give it my all, and the problem is not me. It was from other people who love to bother others and made me feel bad. For a time, I made a mistake and normalized these bad behaviors in others.

Life can be modified by me deciding to heal because it gives me confidence and value in myself. This assessment influenced each of the experiences that I developed in life as an Integrated Individual or a society, that is, the concept we have of ourselves that will make us always choose some things over others, all this opens the way to empathy and the development of social skills, since being emotionally autonomous Involves have the responsibility to respect others.

When I reached adulthood, I believed in the self-knowledge of positive qualities in myself, and how to learn to Identify and manage those emotions that bloom during the activity of self-recognition.

That is why today parents must teach their children to love themselves as they are. And in equal measure striving to improve, and showing them that they can learn from mistakes by facing them is a way to overcome failure.

In conclusion, you have to love yourself, Take care of yourself, Respect yourself, and respect others. Love your neighbor.

Dom Farnan

CEO of DotConnect

https://www.linkedin.com/in/dom-farnan
https://www.instagram.com/iamdomfarnan/
https://www.domfarnan.com
https://www.dotconnectllc.com

For over twenty years, Dom Farnan has been a fearless leader in high-growth settings, blending entrepreneurship and advocacy in each of her roles. Whether she's recruiting talent for titans like Snapchat and Instacart or injecting joy into team meetings through sound and dance, the first thing people notice about Dom is the profound intentionality behind her actions. Dom brings radical change to the talent industry through the application of mindfulness, generosity of spirit, and a sense of compassion that values relationship building.

Currently, she channels her expertise into DotConnect, the conscious connection agency she founded in 2011. In DotConnect's first year of business, Dom scaled the company to $3M. From there, Dom's growth mentality has never subsided. In 2022, DotConnect was honored by being included on the Inc5000 list of the fastest-growing private companies in the country. Dom also founded DoseConnect in 2022, a first-of-its-kind talent company solely focused on psychedelic therapeutics. Blending organizational strategy, systems thinking, and talent acquisition grounded in conscious connection, DoseConnect™ is built to help companies in this space scale for hyper-growth. Working directly with founders, visionaries and high-level operators, the team at DoseConnect™ helps companies with everything from human resources systems and compliance to growth culture transformation.

At home in Southern California, Dom cherishes creating memories with those she loves and is eager to offer a resounding "yes" to new experiences and opportunities. When she's not spending time with her family, Dom can be found collecting stories, writing, and cultivating her soul-affirming spiritual practice. Dom's first book and best seller, "Now Here: A Journey from Toxic Boss to Conscious Connector" is available on Amazon and where books are sold.

EMERGE THROUGH SELF-LOVE

By Dom Farnan

It was in May of 2020 when I had reached a point in my high-functioning depressive lifestyle that I heard the little voice from within that told me, "Enough is enough, it's time to get help". At that point in my life, I didn't really know what that would mean, or what would need to happen, but I knew I could no longer live the way I was living. Until that point, I was living a lie to everyone, but mainly to myself. I would put on the fake smile, or experience the occasional moment of joy, but inside I felt so disconnected from myself, and even worse, my inner dialogue often sounded like that of an angry man, always yelling at me. Barking orders or putting me down. Making me feel small every chance it got. For the longest time, I masked this well. Pretending like I had it all together and that it was "all good". I was very caught up in external validation. Showing the world that I am "good enough" to feel loved and accepted. At the time, of course, I had no idea this was what I was doing.

That summer I began working with my first coach, Angie, and together we slowly started chipping away at the walls I had built around myself and thawing out my heart. I'll admit now that I attempted to do my healing and inner work the same way I approached everything else in my life: with a game plan and action. I didn't leave space for intuition or spiritual guidance. As the months went on, the further I wanted to go on my journey. Questions from within bubbled to the surface, "why am I the way that I am?", "what happened to make me so closed off?", "what am I afraid of?", "who hurt me?", "when did I stop feeling joy?" Even as I write this, I feel my emotions turning inside of me because this is what I've been working through. This is my journey.

From working with Angie to working with other coaches, mentors, and communities, my awareness expanded. I began to leverage breathwork and plant medicine for healing. The funny thing is, until 2021, that had never been something on my radar at all. I prided myself on "being in control" and "never getting out of my head". I laugh about that now, realizing just how much my ego was in the driver's seat. It's through my work with plant medicine that I have been able to reconnect with my soul's essence and feel an overwhelming sense of self-love. But this wasn't easy. This work required me to face off with me. Things I did. Lies I told. Shame, guilt, hurt, ego, and everything in between. There were times on my journey when I wasn't sure how much more I could handle, and yet then I would feel expanded. I would work through so much pain and trauma that I didn't even know I was holding on to, and then I would feel free. I would feel lighter. Creating so much more space in my body for love to pour in. Love from others, but most importantly, love from myself.

I noticed recently that the little voice inside me isn't an angry man yelling at me anymore. It's a soft, gentle, loving voice. Encouraging me, supporting me, acknowledging me. Accepting me for all the things I am, all the things I was, and all the things I long to be. My relationship with myself evolved from what felt like an abusive partnership to a blossoming friendship. I've rebuilt trust with myself by doing things that are uncomfortable or facing fears and knowing that I have everything I need, inside of me, to support me through whatever comes up.

I felt this in my recent work with the grandmother plant, Ayahuasca. It was about 16 months prior that I had sat with her for the first time, in Peru, before I sat again this year in Costa Rica. I'll admit, I was still nervous the second time around. A lot had happened during the time in between. I felt fragile. I began praying the month before my ceremony. In my prayers, I called for support, love, warmth, and forgiveness. I got so much more than that. I went into my ceremony with reverence and openness. I wasn't scared. I had a calm presence and strength from within. My inner guidance so beautifully danced between ego and essence. Tears flowed for hours. It was joyful and freeing. I felt safe inside. My heart felt alive. An overwhelming sense of gratitude for having the courage to confront my demons. The courage to be with whatever grandmother had to show me so I could be free.

In this present moment, I am continuing to witness my rebirth process and I remain open and humble to all the gifts that are for me along the way. Patience, perseverance, and promise are what helped me emerge through self-love and because of that, I am a joyful, free, passionate woman today.

Paula Echeverri

CEO of Neuromomceo

https://www.linkedin.com/in/paulaecheverri/
https://www.instagram.com/themindexplorerceo/
https://www.neuromomceo.com

Paula's journey towards empowerment took her down the path of self-discovery and academic pursuit. She delved into the depths of neuroscience, learning about brainwaves and somatic work that can lead to holistic healing. Armed with knowledge, she overcame anxiety and panic attacks that had gripped her, advocating that true healing stems from understanding the root causes of mental illness. She now helps others do the same in her Neurofit training that combines neuroscience and neurological fitness with the latest technologies in brain health for a strong mind and body.

She have three more books and is passionate advocate of hearing rights in a world that still do not support people with limitations.

Please follow her journey and her Emerge TV show on Fenix TV.

Instagram @neuromomceo
Web: www.neuromomceo.com

LOVE IS THE DOOR, BUT SELF-LOVE IS THE KEY

By Paula Echeverri

Did you know that I am in a relationship with the most wonderful person I ever met?
That makes me happy
That does not mind my flaws or extra pounds
That takes me wherever I want to go, just to awe myself at the sunset
That supports me in every way
And will do everything to make me smile…
That person is MYSELF.

"In the journey of personal growth and self-discovery, one of the most profound and transformative steps we can take is to embrace self-love.

Often overlooked or misunderstood, self-love is not about being narcissistic or selfish. Instead, it's about cultivating a deep sense of compassion, understanding, and acceptance towards oneself. When we truly embrace self-love, we unlock the door to profound healing, inner peace, and the ability to live a fulfilled and authentic life."

What if I tell you SELF-LOVE is the best tool out there for anything in life? You may argue with me, right? You will say no, it's confidence or money or connections or a big house with a car and a dog or having a family.

Many different views and responses, right? But I challenged myself to tell you why it is so important to have it in this book about emerging with SELF-LOVE. I am resting on my couch at my house today sipping a coffee and enjoying the moment. As a writer, I always look for those moments that bring joy and happiness to my life. Looking around I see my dog and a nice view of the sunset out of the window to my patio. I embrace everything and add those moments in the day just when taking my coffee or watching my girls play and laugh which makes me feel at ease.

As the Spanish sun sets over the cityscape of Barcelona, I stand on my patio with my dog, Mochi, taking in the breathtaking view. The journey has been far from easy; I can add any ingredient to the perfect drama if I want to. But every moment of doubt, every hurdle, has led me to this point of fulfillment and success. With a heart full of gratitude, I look forward to the chapters that lie ahead, knowing that I am the author of my own story and that with self-love and unwavering determination, I can overcome any adversity that comes my way.

The Self-Love Project

I am so proud of all the wonderful women here in this book. I am because they believed in this project and themselves. And I would never have imagined that after I went through everything you can think of, checking all the boxes in the list. Physically with illness, mental issues, divorce, failed business ventures, moving to new countries, being alone, and more. Thanks to learning about how to "self-love", surrendering, and accepting myself back again, I turned my life around for good. No matter where I go or who I surround myself with, I know everything will be just fine.

I am so honored to share this with you so you can get there too. You are going to see the storm but also a rainbow at the end. That is all there is in this life; it is all about learning the lessons, and it can get dark and ugly, but from the darkness, there is enlightenment and also learning. You will be successful in life if you learn how to extract the best of any good or bad situation and make your own perfect combination of it.

The Storm in the Sky was in my mind

After writing my first book where I wrote about the challenges I encountered after losing my hearing, I realized I did not write enough about my spiritual life journey too. Which, in fact, was the part of me where I saw more changes during and after my healing process.

Dr. Lisa Miller is a leading psychologist, and scientist on spirituality, mental health, and flourishing. The Columbia Professor and NYT Bestselling Author speaks a lot about this and the awakened brain.

I think that all hard challenges can lead us to enlightenment or awakening. I felt inside of me like something clicked and changed literally in my brain and myself as I hit rock bottom. I was dealing with mental illness from all my struggles because I was not prepared and I was not ready to surrender.

"Dr. Lisa Miller also delves into the profound connection between spirituality, mental health, and the human brain. She addresses the prevalence of dysthymia, depression, and addiction and advocates for a mass awakening to combat these challenges."

My discoveries were profound and reached another level after I decided to embrace that journey. It was a part that was hidden inside of me and that I was not paying enough attention to. I decided to go all the way to researching the brain. I am a researcher and I personally think science and spirituality should go hand-in-hand. The world is now transforming to make a shift in these areas because it is needed.

If you ask me, there are many layers in ourselves that need to be aligned in order to get better health and optimal performance. Those layers for me are physical, mental, and spiritual. I was lacking work in the spiritual aspect, and I believe that was leading to many of my problems physically and mentally. I was trying to live a "regular life" with all that comes with it and not looking at my true, authentic self that was buried under all those layers to the point that I built a fake sense of self.

In our mind, the subconscious mind is where our spirit and even trauma live.

Imagine that those layers are like lenses to see and to feel the world around you and they affect the way we experience things. A person who has been going through trauma or a shocking event in their life does not see the world in the same way people who did not live through the same. So it is up to us to work on those emotions that are bottled up and ready to come out. I was at my breaking point when this happened to me.

"Everything is either an opportunity to grow or an obstacle to keep you from growing. You get to choose." - Wayne Dyer

We blame outside sources for our pains and bad luck, but it is up to us to change the reality we live in. We need to be true to our highest self and we need to look for the answers to love ourselves and others. If you do not love yourself, how can you love others? Think about that. Think about the impact of a mom or parent who has not healed or who thinks they are not enough or don't love themselves much. That impacts our children and their future.

I felt that Self-Love helps us to build resilience, which is our capacity to recover from obstacles. If we know what we need instead of what we want, we can develop meaningful connections with others and align ourselves for a higher purpose. It also comes from our parents and how they teach us to see ourselves and the world. It is a magic recipe for success when we have the right parents who teach us how to value ourselves with kindness and compassion and to create healthy boundaries.

Self-love is an action that we can cultivate where we appreciate ourselves. It is not going to the spa one day; it is something that you develop, a trait that is very useful in life and business.

Social media has changed over the years, but at its core, self-love has evolved and declined from generation to generation, making us more prone to forget to cultivate those elements that lead to a healthier and happier life.

Let me tell you, it is not easy. Everyone has a different perception and that could differ from yours. As I was younger I would go in life looking for external gratification like love. I thought finding the best partner would fix my life but it did not. I married a great person and a good friend and later divorced after years of marriage. Thanks to my process during my marriage and the physical problems that I developed, over time I found out that all I needed was inside of me. I needed to be the best version of myself I could be at that moment.

I spent a lot of alone time finding the answers, **but not until I became deaf did I start to understand my true purpose, my vision, and how to lead an authentic life** based on the principles that I set for myself. I was not settling for less. I saw myself in another light, a more compassionate light, that led me to understand I was enough and that I am all I need to be happy.

I started noticing subtle changes in my mindset and how I saw life. If depression or hard moments in life set you on the path of a spiritual awakening, then I guess this is how I would define mine. I am not here to claim that I am a spiritual guru by any means, but I feel in my heart and soul that I need to share some hard truths to help people in their journey. If that makes a difference, then that is fantastic, and if not, I understand now not everyone will get what I am living as everyone lives their way based on what they believe.

When I hit rock bottom I decided to EMERGE and work hard and diligently for the new, improved version that I built. In the process, I lost a lot of people that I cared about, but I understand that I was not aligned with their life purpose anymore. Building myself and my self-love was a hard process that is still occurring every day. I have the foundations that I built, but I do put a bit more into every day in everything I do trying to be the most authentic person I can be. I come from a lineage of women who did not speak their minds and purpose. I had to speak because that healed my wounds and made me a better person.

The discovery of a lifetime!

Some people may ask, what is the secret of life? Well, for me in this life, the universe set me on a discovery path and I am focused on getting the most in my spiritual journey, always being strategic and making the right decisions to protect my energy but at the same time opening my heart and being vulnerable. One of my biggest changes was that I was living in a mindset of looking for outside pleasures. I reflected on this so much because what **I really needed was to understand that I was just one with the universe.**

This oneness turned my life and mindset around in a way I cannot explain! I now feel connected to the world and being true to myself. I think it is the most powerful thing that I have discovered in my journey yet. Why? Because it forced me to see life totally differently, like everyone was on their own journey and that is ok. Even people who were mean or not kind to me I started to see in another light. A light that showed me that their path was to test me in my journey and their unkindness was their learning too. I did not take it personally and I realized we are all in this evolving environment called EARTH where we play based on rules set before we are born.

We are always looking for what we want. Instead you need to look for what you need.

The wants are what will give instant gratification, but do we really need them?

When you start to get clarity about your needs, the plan of action is easier and you start making sure you get there because it is what you really need to get your goals and be happy.

I changed who I was for a better version of myself but I have not changed my true essence, my soul, and my vision which was always very altruistic and empathetic to the suffering of all humans and animals. I had it in my heart to try to help others, and this feeling got bigger in a way that I still cannot believe after I went through all those obstacles. It is hard to explain, but I started to see things in a different way. I was trying to understand the why, MY WHY, and I embraced it all with open arms because I just could not deny it anymore. I changed.

It could be scary at first, to be honest. Did you read the *Divine Comedy* from Dante Alighieri? I was obsessed with that book when I was younger, and life for me feels a little bit like that. A chain of events and places where you go through life being tested. Hell, Purgatory, and Paradise are places where you can either suffer or have joy depending on the way you see things.

Unfortunately, we live in roles in a society that keeps feeding us what to consume and how to behave. It is really hard to grow like this today. Especially after being attached to our devices all day.

A major thing for me was to learn to be comfortable with the uncomfortable emotions that I had inside of me, eating me, and I tried so hard to bury them. Feelings of not being adequate or valued for having a limitation.

"There is an actual process of living with neutrality as I call it or living in the flow."

At first, it makes you feel uncomfortable just being a spectator of your own feelings and emotions that move through your body, but with practice, I have achieved great results that lead to permanent changes in my life and body.

Just accepting and surrendering to the uncomfortable emotions and letting them be, befriending them, and observing them. Then I practice somatic movements that help me reset the nervous system that I have in my bag of tools. I personally love tapping, jumping, or using my logic, just asking questions like, "where is this coming from?" or "where do I feel it?" and analyzing why it is happening (as many people imagine things that are not real, leading to anxiety).

Give your anxiety a name; for example, name her Lily and every time it comes to your body, look where you feel it, identify it, and ask: "What do you want from me, Lily?" Think about the emotion and listen to your body and mind as many things may come up. Separate YOURSELF from the emotion and let it flow through your body. We need to feel safe in our bodies.

"By doing this process you can lower the impact of your emotions and they become less uncomfortable in your body."

I even use it with my daughter who used to trigger me a lot in the past. Now I see her emotions and I try to stay as a spectator without letting her affect me.

The impermanence does not stress me anymore as I do not live in fear because I work every day in my nervous system for my mental and physical health. I sprinkle this wisdom wherever I can with my clients and even with my kids. But I do add "sparks" of joy to my day in my mindfulness journey where I find value in every little moment; look for those sparks in your day. For me, my morning coffee sitting on my couch or just watching my kids be silly and play… find many of those and be grateful for having them.

It was not always like this. There was a time when I clung desperately to the idea of permanence, seeking security in a world that was constantly shifting. The fear of losing loved ones, of facing the unknown, and of change itself would keep me awake at night, my heart racing with anxiety. But life has a way of teaching us valuable lessons, and in my case, it was through the passage of time and the wisdom gained from experiences.

One evening, as I watched the sun sink lower in the sky, I realized that I had reached a point where I no longer cared about the evanescence of life. It was a liberating feeling, like shedding a heavy coat that I had been carrying for years. I had discovered that by surrendering to the flow of life, I gained a sense of control that I had never experienced before— control over my reactions, my emotions, and my perspective.

I believe problems are a blessing in our lives and they pivot us to change and grow because we are yearning for it internally.

We are supposed to take problems as opportunities. I know it could be hard but after some time you will start seeing that your divorce, illness, or any trouble was sending you to a better place.

This is how we need to show kids to be resilient and comfortable so they can become better humans who enjoy being challenged and not defeated by a problem or an obstacle. **If we look at things and reframe our human experience, then our perception changes.**

The Power of Your Intuition

When I speak about self-love we need to talk about our intuition. Why? Because if we are connected with our intuition we are always going to do the best for ourselves. We will love ourselves and demand from others the value we truly deserve.

When you connect with your intuition you connect with love, and that is what I did. My journey showed me that I needed to get in touch with my heart and soul to ultimately love myself and therefore love others too. The problem is that we confuse our intuition with our inferior mind, which is the ego. The ego is your life experience and is always there to judge or make you feel small and safe. I called my ego my "whiny child" and that makes me feel less attached to it.

Connecting with our intuition is a remarkable and often underestimated source of power in our lives. Intuition, often referred to as our inner wisdom or gut feeling, is an innate ability that resides within each of us. It's the subtle whisper of our subconscious mind, guiding us toward making better decisions and navigating the complexities of life.

Here is my secret: when **you live in neutrality, you activate your intuition.** That's why it is so important to live practicing mindfulness as it opens the portal to just being in that neutrality that is so powerful.

Connecting with our intuition can be a source of inner peace and confidence. It allows us to trust ourselves and our abilities, reducing self-doubt and anxiety. When we follow our intuitive guidance, we often find ourselves on a path that feels authentic and aligned with our purpose, leading to a greater sense of fulfillment and contentment in life.

For the more spiritual, your connection with your pituitary gland (called the Third Eye) helps you to do this as well. I am still on a journey of discovery as I have been a researcher, looking for the "why", but my connection with myself has improved. It is my superpower now to connect to this and to be who I am authentically.

There is no right or wrong in each person's journey because it is your own and nobody else's. Live with an open heart and as authentically as you can so your intuition will be the compass that will guide you.

I am finishing this chapter today in my journey and this moment of writing will lead me to a purpose through shining my light as much as I can, giving you the best, to make sure you can become what you are destined to be in this life. I am sipping soup right now and this makes me feel good, but I am wondering why I feel like eating soup when it's a hot summer day. Well, I did eat it because I followed what my body and my soul needed.

Sometimes life is like that; people will ask you why or judge you. However, it is your journey, not theirs. So keep doing what makes your heart and soul sing like my soup on a hot summer day.

If everyone understood that concept, life would be so much easier today!

I am right here for you or on social media under neuromomceo where I share my own personal wisdom with the world.

Remember, life is not about the special moments, it is about finding the extraordinary out of the ordinary!

Love, Paula Echeverri

Dr. Angela Butts Chester

DR ANGELA CHESTER
Pastoral Counselor, Media Entrepreneur, and
International Women's Speaker

https://www.linkedin.com/in/drangelachester/
https://www.facebook.com/DrAngelaChester/
https://www.instagram.com/drangelachester/
https://www.drangelachester.com/
https://www.passionairemag.com/

Dr. Angela Butts Chester is unwavering about transforming the lives of faith-centered purpose-driven women all around the world.

A Pastoral Counselor in private practice, this author, cancer survivor, and host of talk radio show Daily Spark with Dr. Angela and its award-winning sister show, Daily Spark TV, has built a career spanning more than 20 years and hundreds and thousands of people counseled.

Dr. Chester has also served as an Associate Pastor and has built a reputation as a thought leader on issues related to Women's Health and Wellness (spiritual) and Women's Empowerment as an International Motivational Speaker.

As Editor-in-Chief of PASSIONAIRE Magazine, this bi-monthly magazine features articles on lifestyle + passion for purpose. Dr. Angela also provides a weekly space for women in leadership to have a positive voice for change on PASSIONAIRE Magazine The Podcast.

LOVE IS THE ANTIDOTE: OVERCOMING FEAR WITH FAITH

By Dr. Angela Butts Chester

Humans have two main emotions – fear and love. We operate from these two base emotions daily without thinking about it. We process our decisions through their filters. Will you or won't you? Stop or go. Say yes or respectfully decline. Psychology says that love is the strongest emotion, although humans experience a range from happiness to fear and anger. Anger with its strong dopamine response is not more profound, more intense, or life-changing than that of love.

Speaking of chemical reactions, when it comes to relationships, oxytocin is a chemical that gives us that ecstatic feeling associated with love. It also triggers us to feel concerned over things that may go wrong. Over the years we have been better able to determine what is truly a concern and what isn't. Think about new first-time parents. They are doing all they can to make sure that they give their little one the best possible environment, one that is safe and free from harm. Fast forward to the parent with three children. The newest little one will have a different experience in some ways because the parent has learned how to maneuver. They now have the wisdom and experience of a seasoned parent. They have figured out how to operate from a different place; they have learned to not solely operate from fear.

As sure as the sun will rise in the morning, fear will try to pop its head into your life from time to time. Adding a layer of faith to your *carpe diem* adds a coating of amour to your emotional personal protection plan. By doing so, you make it harder for fear and faith to coexist at the same time. But let's face it, we're human, so we do human things. That means we can have faith in God, God's plan for us, and God's plan for the world but still struggle with our very human fears. Our fears are our insecurities which, at their core, can always be traced back to a fundamental fear or a feeling of a lack of love in some area.

Overcoming fear with faith is a powerful tool that can change our lives. When we learn to trust in something greater than ourselves, we can find the courage to face our fears and move forward. The key ingredient needed is love. Love can help us make this transition like none other. Here are some ways in which love can help us overcome our fears:

- Love can provide us with a sense of security and comfort. When we feel loved, we know that we are not alone and that we have someone who cares for us. This can give us the strength to face our fears and take action.

- Love can help us to see the good in others and in ourselves. When we focus on the positive qualities of those around us, we are less likely to be consumed by fear and negativity. Similarly, when we love ourselves, we are more likely to believe in our own abilities and to take risks.

- Love can inspire us to be our best selves. When we are motivated by love, we are more likely to act with kindness, compassion, and generosity. These qualities can help us to overcome our fears and to create positive change in the world.

- Love can teach us to forgive. When we hold onto grudges and resentment, we are often held back by fear and anger. However, when we learn to forgive ourselves and others, we can release these negative emotions and move forward with faith and hope.

This transition all starts with self-love. Self-love can be hard for some. They feel loving themselves is selfish, when in fact, you must love yourself first in order to properly love another.

So, stop comparing yourself to others. It's easy to fall into the trap of comparing ourselves to others, especially in today's, social media-obsessed world. Realize that everyone's journey is different. Do your best.

Practice self-care. Take care of yourself. Make sure to get enough sleep, exercise regularly, and eat healthy. Make time for activities that bring you joy, such as reading and spending time with loved ones.

Learn to say no. Say no to things that don't align with your values or goals.

Embrace your imperfections. Instead of trying to hide your flaws, learn to embrace them. Your imperfections make you unique, and that's something to be celebrated. When we look at the Bible stories we learned as children, we see they are regular people. They talk about the imperfect people God used in His perfect plan.

By incorporating more love into our lives, we can transform our fears into opportunities for growth and transformation. Whether we are facing a challenging situation or simply trying to navigate the ups and downs of daily life, love can be a powerful force that helps us overcome our fears and live with greater purpose and meaning.

One way we can reassure those we love is by listening. Listening is a valuable asset in any relationship. Parent to child, partner to partner, spouse to spouse, co-worker to co-worker.

In today's fast-paced world, it's easy to forget the importance of truly listening to one another. As a pastoral counselor, I've seen firsthand the power of couples learning to listen with love and attention. Let me explain.

Listening is an act of love. When we truly listen to someone, we show them that they are valued and heard. This can be a powerful form of love and can help build deeper connections and understanding between people. This is especially true for someone who grew up in a family where they never felt seen or understood. If we think about our own conversations, the back-and-forth makes for a great time. No one likes a conversation hog.

Listening requires patience. It's easy to get distracted or want to interrupt someone when they're speaking, but true listening requires patience. We need to give the other person enough time to express themselves fully before we respond.

Listening means paying attention to nonverbal cues. When we listen, we need to pay attention not just to what the other person is saying, but also to their nonverbal cues. This includes things like their tone of voice, facial expressions, and body language. These cues can give us important insights into how the other person is feeling.

Listening means setting aside our own biases; it's important to approach each conversation with an open mind and without judgment. We need to set aside our own biases and perspectives in order to truly understand where the other person is coming from.

Listening can be healing. Sometimes, all someone needs is to be heard. By listening to someone, we can help them feel seen and understood. This can be incredibly healing and can help build trust.

Listening with love is a powerful tool that can help us build deeper connections with others and create a more compassionate world. By being patient with others and ourselves, paying attention to nonverbals, setting aside our biases, and truly hearing others, we can become better listeners and people.

I've also been the recipient of great listening skills. My oncology team was great at listening to me when I was dealing with breast cancer. During such an emotionally high time in my life, knowing that when it was time to meet with them, I wasn't just another patient. I was made to feel secure in their abilities. Sure, they could've spent 15 minutes with me and moved on, but instead they asked about me.

They remembered the small details from the last appointment and followed up. Did you get to the park like you wanted to last time? You started taking your meds at night instead of in the morning – did that help with any side effects? Sure, they were just doing their jobs, and have been taught to pay attention to the details; however, not everyone has the same experience even when going through the same medical condition.

The power of listening isn't just limited to the people around us. As a person of faith, I believe that God listens to us with the same intensity and focus. Many of you have heard me talk about the importance of my life verse – Jeremiah 29:11.

Jeremiah 29:11 states, "For I know the plans I have for you, declares the Lord, plans for welfare and not for evil, to give you a future and a hope." These words became my guiding light during my battle with breast cancer. Instead of succumbing to anxiety, worry, depression, or despair, I chose faith over fear, believing that there was a greater purpose behind the obstacle before me. I turned to self-care to keep myself in high spirits.

My godmother gave me a "just because" card one day when I was sixteen that included the verse on the inside. That day, the scripture spoke to my heart and I've never put it down since. Jeremiah 29:11 became my mantra, a constant reminder that God had a plan for me, even in the face of medical adversity. So, I, in turn, continued to walk in the love of God, choosing to listen to His words repeat in my spirit.

My journey through cancer treatment was arduous, but my unwavering faith and positive outlook now serve as a beacon of hope for others. By sharing my story as a speaker - both the joys and concerns – others see that they are not alone as they travel the same road to becoming a survivor of breast cancer. I shine a light as a survivor and pastoral counselor in the darkest of times for others providing a spark of hope during very trying and uncertain times for many. By providing them with a safe place to offload, it allows them the hope to continue to move forward.

After successfully overcoming breast cancer, I continued to walk in my calling to help others heal spiritually and emotionally as a pastoral counselor. My passion for helping others has been a driving force in my life, and I find fulfillment walking in this purpose. Through my work, I understand the importance of providing a safe and non-judgmental space for individuals to share their struggles and receive support. I provide a place for them to put down their emotional bags of fear and pick up the love provided by faith. I teach them that it's okay to take time for themselves through self-care. You can not pour from an empty cup.

Pastoral counselors especially recognize the importance of spirituality in the healing process. We help those who have experienced trauma heal according to their faith and where they are along that path. We utilize a variety of techniques, including mindfulness practices, to help individuals process and move through their trauma with grace and dignity. Having overcome my own experience of trauma (chemotherapy, surgery, and radiation) I am uniquely equipped to support others in their healing journeys.

Perhaps you are someone who loves to read. I believe that authors and readers have a special relationship. A reader appreciates the words of the author as they take them along the pages of their work. Authors appreciate readers as they receive rave reviews of their work and see the sales skyrocket. My love of books and reading also have a special place in my life. I've created a space for both readers and authors to gather.

I am blessed to have a radio and TV show, a magazine, and a podcast as a media entrepreneur where I provide a platform for women to gather. To learn from one another and share their stories of pain and sorrows, of joys and successes, of re-dos and outtakes.

Looking to scripture again for inspiration John 3:16, one of the most well-known and Googled verses, reminds us that God so loved the world that He gave his only Son for it. That means all genders, ethnicities, and races equally. Women and men, alike. So, my entrepreneurial spirit led me to establish a media platform dedicated to empowering women. Through this venture, I created spaces for women to share their stories, voices, and experiences. These media endeavors not only provided a platform for women's empowerment but also showcased my love and commitment to uplifting others and allowed women personal permission to just be themselves and love who she is, thus helping them find their voices.

I believe there is no such thing as happenstance. That when we pray, God hears us, and like a loving parent, provides for His children accordingly. With this understanding, the Christian love we experience is likened to that of a family. So, when I serve as a women's empowerment coach, I am my sister's keeper. I am living out the mandate of Romans 2:10 "Love one another with brotherly affection and outdo one another in showing honor."

The coaching programs focus on helping women realize their full potential, overcome obstacles, and embrace their unique gifts and talents. Many women have never had someone believe in them or encourage them without an ulterior motive.

Just like the woman at the well, so many women have had to make choices according to their needs at the time instead of what brings them joy and honor. But faith allows us to reshape ourselves and our lives in a way that shows love to others and ourselves. It reassures us. It reminds us that as we have been chosen, so we are called, to different jobs, vocations, careers, and paths to ensure the right people are in the right place at the right time. Hurry along too quickly and you may miss the person you're hoping for because you were too early. Go too slowly and they have arrived and already departed due to time restraints. Coaching helps you find the right mode of transportation for each of life's endeavors.

I love the life I have been given. Every day I understand more and more. I see further and wider. I hear more clearly and with more wisdom the words shared with me. My life's journey is a testament to the transformative power of faith, love, and purpose. My battle with breast cancer, guided by Jeremiah 29:11, serves as a reminder that adversity can be a stepping stone to greater things. Through pastoral counseling, media entrepreneurship, and women's empowerment coaching, I continue to shine a light, inspiring others to do the same.

Life is a complex weave of emotions and experiences. We encounter threads of love and fear, of hope and gratitude, and of listening and being heard. Learn to use the tools that you have been given to the best of your ability and to their highest power and intention. Love one another as you love yourself. Give to someone else as you would want them to give to you. Take care of yourself as you are the temple of God.

By leading your life with pure love as your guiding principle, not only will you achieve your goals, but you'll also inspire others along the way. So, let me leave you with this call to action:

Live a life of improved relationships. Approach all your interactions with love and kindness. When you do, you are more likely to build strong, positive relationships with others. This can lead to a happier and more fulfilling life.

Live life with empathy. Love allows us to understand and relate to others on a deeper level. When we lead with love, we are more likely to be empathetic to those around us, which can improve our communication both as the one speaking and listening.

Live life with greater inner peace. When you approach life with love, you are less likely to hold onto negative emotions such as anger or resentment. This can lead to a greater sense of inner peace and contentment.

Live a productive life. When you approach your work with love and passion, you are more likely to be productive and successful. Love can inspire us to do our best work and to strive for excellence in all areas of our lives.

Live a life that leaves a positive impact on the world. When we lead with love, we have the power to inspire and uplift others. By spreading love and kindness, we can create a ripple effect that can positively impact the world around us.

Remember, leading with love is not always easy, and it may not always be the most popular or convenient choice. But by choosing love as your guiding principle, you can live a more fulfilling and meaningful life for yourself and others.

Rose Mendes

Founder and CEO of Brazilian Body Care

https://www.linkedin.com/in/rose-mendes-9b7433199/
https://www.instagram.com/rosebbcmendes/
https://www.brazilianbodycare.com/

Rose Mendes, beautician, cosmetologist and dietitian, arrives in Barcelona for Brazilian Body Care, a beauty center and boutique where the benefits of the exotic and natural from Brazil are merged with the avant-garde and innovative cosmetology from France, a new concept to the traditional offer.

She with more than 25 years of experience dedicated to body and facial aesthetics, she is a cosmetologist in health and well-being. Rose began her professional career at the prestigious Jacques Jannie chain in the city of Sao Paulo. Due to her talent, she was invited to open a beauty center in Lisbon by the renowned hairdresser Joao Chaves.

After dedicating herself to the world of hairdressing, aesthetics and fashion, she decides to enter the world of hospitality, spa and wellness, giving professional training in the Canary Islands. Finally, in 2017, she decided to translate her entire trajectory and her concept of well-being to Barcelona to create an aesthetic, health and well-being center called Brazilian Body Care.

BEAUTY IS A WORK INSIDE AND OUTSIDE

By Rose Mendes

The streets of Barcelona whispered tales of passion and resilience as the city bathed in the golden glow of the setting sun. It was here that I had chosen to create my sanctuary of wellness and self-love, a testament to my journey from a motherless teenager filled with sadness to a thriving CEO and professional beauty guru.

As a child, I experienced a loss that carved deep into my heart, one that no amount of time could ever completely fill. I lost my mother at a young age, and her absence left me feeling abandoned in a world that often seemed indifferent to my pain. My emotional teenage years had been particularly challenging due to a natural rebellion from that phase of life, but also because I was trying to find myself in the middle of the storm.

Losing a loved one, especially a parent like your mom, can be an incredibly challenging and emotional experience. It's entirely natural to have a range of emotions and thoughts in the aftermath of such a loss, including a heightened sense of responsibility for taking care of yourself.

It was during those formative years that I learned the reality of judgment and misunderstanding. People around me, blissfully unaware of my internal struggles, often dismissed me as distant. They couldn't know the depth of my sadness or the well of frustration that surged within me. I felt like an outsider, caught in a whirlwind of emotions I couldn't express.

One day, I overheard a conversation that cut deeper than any other. "Always so quiet, like she's got some secret she's hiding," I fought to contain my emotions. I had always strived to be a good person, to be kind and empathetic to others. Yet, these words stung, serving as a painful reminder that without knowing, a deep, strong feeling inside of me made me dedicate my life to excellence in anything I tried.

I was determined to use that pain as fuel for my journey of self-discovery. I knew that if I couldn't change the opinions of those around me, at least I could change myself. I would find my purpose and my passion, and I would channel my emotions into something positive and beautiful.

In the years that followed, I immersed myself in the world of wellness and beauty. I learned the art of massage from the best in the industry, even working with celebrities in the Brazilian space. I was honing my skills to perfection and became an expert in skincare, beauty techniques, and nutrition.

Each day, as my hands moved with grace and precision, I could feel the frustration and sadness flow away, replaced by a sense of calm and purpose. I put my heart and soul into every job, every customer, and every person I met opening myself to give the best experience I could offer so they will see my commitment to change one woman at a time.

After completing my training, I decided to follow my heart to Barcelona. The vibrant city offered me a fresh start, a canvas upon which I could paint my dreams. I opened my own wellness and beauty business, a place where I could excel in my services and share the power of self-love and self-care with others.

My Brazilian influence and roots are part of my work of enhancing women's natural beauty. My new concept was a hit, and it was an honor and tribute to the joy and passion of people and landscapes from Brazil. I do bring my love for my country as part of what I do and that shows in every step of my journey.

"In Brazil, there isn't just one beauty ideal.
There's a lot of emphasis on a woman's natural beauty – but of course,
Brazilian women love expressing their beauty through makeup."
— Adriana Lima

Barcelona embraced me with open arms, and my clientele grew steadily. People from all walks of life sought solace and rejuvenation in Brazilian Body Care, my sanctuary. But my mission went beyond just providing exceptional services. I wanted to teach others the importance of self-care, of embracing their own beauty, inside and out.

I held workshops and trained people to do my unique protocol which I developed through the years and want to pass some secrets to you in this book too but always supporting others and sharing my story of transformation and resilience with my clients.

I discovered that wellness and self-love are closely interconnected, and they can have a profound impact on each other.

Here's how they are connected:

Physical Health: Taking care of your physical health is an act of self-love. This includes eating nutritious foods, engaging in regular physical activity, getting enough sleep, and avoiding harmful habits like smoking or excessive alcohol consumption. When you prioritize your physical health, you are demonstrating self-love by ensuring that your body is functioning at its best, which can lead to improved overall wellness.

Mental Health: Self-love plays a significant role in mental wellness. Practicing self-compassion and self-acceptance with yourself and your body no matter your size can help you manage stress, anxiety, and depression more effectively. When you love and accept yourself, you are less likely to engage in negative self-talk or be overly critical, which can lead to better mental health.

Emotional Health: Self-love involves acknowledging and honoring your emotions. It means allowing yourself to feel your feelings without judgment and expressing them in healthy ways. When you practice self-love in this way, you are more likely to have healthier emotional well-being and relationships with others.

Self-Care: Self-love is often expressed through self-care activities. Engaging in self-care routines such as having a massage, taking a relaxing bath, meditating, or pursuing hobbies you enjoy, can boost your overall wellness. These practices are a way of showing yourself that you are worthy of time and attention.

Resilience: Self-love can enhance your ability to bounce back from challenges and setbacks. When you love and believe in yourself, you are more likely to persevere and maintain a positive outlook, even in difficult situations. This resilience contributes to your overall wellness by helping you navigate life's ups and downs more effectively.

Healthy Boundaries: Self-love involves setting and maintaining healthy boundaries in your relationships and life. This helps prevent burnout and stress, contributing to better overall wellness. When you prioritize your own needs and well-being, you can show up as a healthier and happier person in your interactions with others.

Motivation for Positive Change: When you truly love and care for yourself, you are more motivated to make positive changes in your life. This might include seeking personal growth, pursuing meaningful goals, or making choices that align with your values. These actions can lead to an enhanced sense of purpose and well-being.

I think it is very important to project an image and reflect what is inside your heart. I love getting ready in the morning and looking sharp. It makes me happy and motivated and sends a message to others that I care and indeed love myself. It is a ritual in every little thing from how you take care of your skin to what you eat that really reflects if you love yourself or not. Many people call this now "well-aging" and I think it is important to reflect on that.

I also enjoy connecting with all kinds of women besides my clients at events and fostering a wonderful community around me everywhere I go. This helps me make valuable friendships that are close to my heart. The value of women supporting each other is key to my success and being who I am.

> *"When women support each other, incredible things happen."*
> —Viola Davis

So what are my secrets? If you ask me about Brazilian beauty secrets I would reply "confidence", which is perhaps the most important beauty secret of all. Brazilians often embrace their natural beauty and radiate confidence, which is considered very attractive no matter your age or size. Brazilians really have a joy for living too that is infectious.

But I want to share with you some of my secrets here that I personally use with me.

This is seven days of the 7-day menu that I created for wellness and longevity (which is originally 14 but try this for now). Even a kid can do it because it is healthy and if done as it says is a great weight loss tool.

ULTRA MENU DETOX

Menu - Day 1

Breakfast
- 1 glass of Detox juice (1 cabbage leaf, 1 small slice of melon, 100 ml of water, ¼ of squeezed lemon and 4 mint leaves)
- ½ papaya, with 1 tablespoon of flax seeds
- 1 cup of green tea

Midmorning
- 150 ml of coconut water or 1 slice of melon

Meal
- Lettuce salad, arugula, raw cabbage (to taste), ½ grated carrot and ½ tomato
- 2 tablespoons of brown rice
- 1 grilled chicken filet

Snack
- 1 cup of hibiscus infusion or green tea
- 3 cashews or Pará chestnuts (Brazil nuts)

Dinner
- 1 deep plate of vegetables sautéed with garlic and olive oil, which can also be prepared as a soup (1 cup of tea of each of the following ingredients: cabbage, broccoli, cauliflower, and cabbage). Add 1 tablespoon of coconut oil and 1/3 cup of celery. Season preferably with: pepper, garlic, and onion.

Dinner
- 1 cup of chamomile with 1 thread of honey
- 3 cashews or Pará chestnuts (Brazil nuts)

Menu - Day 2

Breakfast
- 1 glass of Detox juice (1 small stalk of celery, 1 cabbage leaf, 1 slice of pineapple, 150 ml of water and a trickle of honey)
- ½ papaya, with 1 tablespoon of flax seeds
- 1 cup of green tea

Midmorning
- 1 glass of melon juice with 1 slice of pineapple

Meal

- Lettuce, chard, or arugula salad (to taste) and 2 stems of steamed cauliflower
- 2 grilled fish or chicken filets
- 2 tablespoons of brown rice
- 2 tablespoons of black beans with curry

Snack

- 1 glass of Detox juice (150 ml of green tea, 1 medium slice of melon, 1 tablespoon tureen of linseed seeds, 1 thread of honey and ice). Take cold
- 2 cashews or Pará chestnuts (Brazil nuts)

Dinner

- 1 deep bowl of soup (2 cups of cabbage, 1 cup of spinach or cabbage, 1 cup of pumpkin, 1 tablespoon of coconut oil, 1 pinch of curry and water). Boil all ingredients until they become soft, if you prefer you can beat everything in the blender.
  Season preferably with: pepper, garlic, and onion.

Dinner

- 1 cup of chamomile with 1 teaspoon of cinnamon

Menu - Day 3

Breakfast

- 1 Detox juice (1 apple, 3 strawberries, ½ squeezed lemon, 150 ml of coconut water or water, and 1 teaspoon of flax seeds)
- 1 portion of light fresh cheese
- 1 cup of green tea

Midmorning

- 1 slice of pineapple with 1 tablespoon of flax seeds

Meal

- Lettuce, chard, and cabbage salad (to taste) and 2 slices of tomato
- 2 cooked chicken filets with 2 cups of cabbage
- 2 tablespoons of brown rice
- 2 tablespoons of black beans with curry

Snack

- 1 cup of hibiscus infusion or green tea
- 1 slice of pineapple

Dinner

- 1 deep bowl of soup (1 cup of beet, 1 cup of onion, 1 clove of garlic, 1 tablespoon of coconut oil and water). Boil everything, and beat in the blender. Align preferably with pepper, garlic, and onion.
- 1 shallow plate of raw spinach and cabbage leaf salad with olive oil
- 1 boiled egg

Dinner

- 1 chopped apple with 1 teaspoon of cinnamon

Menu – Day 4

Breakfast

- 1 Detox juice (1 small carrot, 4 strawberries, 1 small piece of watermelon, 1 tablespoon soup of chia and 150 ml of water)
- 1 portion of light fresh cheese
- 1 cup of green tea

Midmorning

- 1 small slice of watermelon
- 2 cashews or Pará chestnuts (Brazil nuts)

Meal

- Lettuce and spinach salad (to taste), ½ grated carrot and ½ beet
- 2 tablespoons of brown rice
- 1 tablespoon sautéed pumpkin puree
- 1 grilled fish or chicken filet

Snack

- 1 yogurt (zero fat) with 3 strawberries and 1 tablespoon of chia

Dinner

- 1 deep plate of vegetables sautéed with garlic and olive oil, which can also be prepared as a soup (1 cup of each of the following ingredients: cabbage, broccoli, cauliflower, and cabbage). Add 1 tablespoon coconut oil and 1/3 cup celery. Season preferably with pepper, garlic, and onion

Dinner

- 1 cup of chamomile with 1 teaspoon of cinnamon

Menu – Day 5

Breakfast

- 1 Detox juice (½ lemon, 3 strawberries, 2 large slices of watermelon, and 100 ml of water)
- ½ papaya, with 1 tablespoon of flax seeds
- 1 cup of green tea

Midmorning

- 150 ml of coconut water or 1 slice of watermelon

Meal

- Lettuce and chard salad (to taste) and 1 cup of sautéed broccoli
- 1 tablespoon of pumpkin puree sautéed with garlic and olive oil

- 2 tablespoons of brown rice
- 1 grilled chicken filet

Snack
- 1 glass of Detox juice (green tea, 1 squeezed orange, ½ carrot and ice). Take cold.

Dinner
- 1 deep soup bowl (1 cup of pumpkin, 1 cup of carrot, 1 clove of garlic, 1 tablespoon of coconut oil and water). Boil everything and beat in the blender. Align preferably with pepper, garlic, and onion
- 1 shallow plate of raw lettuce and cabbage leaf salad with olive oil

Dinner
- 1 cup of chamomile with honey.

Menu – Day 6

Breakfast
- 1 Detox juice (3 cabbage leaves, 1 tablespoon of chia, ½ apple, 150 ml of water, and a thread of honey)
- ½ papaya
- 1 cup of green tea

Midmorning
- 1 slice of melon
- 2 cashews or Pará chestnuts (Brazil nuts)

Meal
- Lettuce and cabbage salad (to taste) and 2 slices of tomato
- 1 sliced roasted eggplant with olive oil and oregano
- 2 tablespoons of brown rice

- 1 roasted chicken thigh

Snack
- 1 cup of hibiscus infusion or green tea
- ½ apple

Dinner
- 1 deep bowl of soup (2 cups of cabbage, 1 cup of carrot, 1 cup of pumpkin, ½ cup of celery, 1 tablespoon of coconut oil, 1 pinch of curry and water). Boil all the ingredients until they are soft, if you prefer you can beat everything in the blender. Add 2 tablespoons shredded chicken. Preferably align with pepper, garlic, and onion.

Dinner
- 1 cup of chamomile with 1 teaspoon of cinnamon

Menu – Day 7

Breakfast
- 1 Detox juice (2 slices of melon, 3 cabbage leaves, 1 tablespoon of chia, 150 ml of water, and a trickle of honey)
- 1 yogurt (zero fat)
- 1 cup of green tea

Midmorning
- 1 slice of melon

Meal
- Salad with lettuce, watercress, cabbage, chard (to taste) and 2 slices of tomato
- 2 tablespoons of brown rice
- 2 shredded chicken filets
- 2 tablespoons of spinach sautéed with garlic and olive oil

Snack

- 1 glass of Detox juice (green tea, 2 slices of melon and ice). Take cold.

Dinner

- 1 deep plate of vegetables sautéed with garlic and olive oil, which can also be prepared as a soup (1 cup of each of the following ingredients: cabbage, watercress, cabbage, and broccoli). Add 1 tablespoon of coconut oil and 1 pinch of curry.
  Season preferably with: pepper, garlic, and onion
- 1 boiled egg

Dinner

- 1 cup of chamomile with 1 thread of honey
- 3 cashews or Pará chestnuts (Brazil nuts)

Tips and recommendations

1- Salt to taste

You can add salt to the recipes, in moderation.

However, it is advisable to give preference to natural dressings such as onion, garlic, and pepper.

2- No sugar or alcohol.

During the DETOX process, eliminate sugar! You can use honey only as a sweetener.

3- Drink plenty of water

Remember: you are detoxifying and toxins need to be eliminated.

This only happens with the help of water (2 to 2.5 liters per day).

4- Don't ignore your body's signals

Pay attention to pain, hunger, and thirst. If you get hungry, eat chestnuts and fruit, and drink plenty of water. Preferably, eat the following fruits in the first days: watermelon, melon, papaya, pineapple, and strawberries.

In case of any symptoms, see a doctor.

The Ultra DETOX menu only lasts 7 days. Stay strong! I developed this and more protocols for my clients that work. With this detox diet, you will feel better and you can lose two to five kilos of weight if you follow the food plan as it is.

I have a lot more recipes and protocols that I plan to publish in my next book that I use on myself, my family, and my clients. I have overcome my past, healing and using my pain and frustration as stepping stones to reach the pinnacle of my profession.

My dream for this book is to put my story out there, and I really hope that my journey from a motherless teenager to a thriving entrepreneur was an inspiration to all who crossed my path and inspires them to never give up. I want to inspire women in general and all generations that cross my path using beauty as my magical wand to heal and ease any worries, so they can feel their best inside and out to achieve any dreams and goals just like I did.

> *"Because a challenge is just a little rock in the road not a sentence for failure."*

Recognizing that we don't have all the answers and that we can learn from our mistakes is a sign of wisdom. Problems can humble us and remind us that there is always more to learn and discover.

As the sun dipped below the horizon, casting a warm glow over my bustling spa, I looked around with a sense of contentment. I had not only overcome my own barriers but also helped countless others in their journey towards self-acceptance and self-love. Barcelona has become a haven of healing, a place where roses can bloom even amidst thorns.

Love and health, Rose.

Paola Montes

Founder of Glam & Aesthetics

https://www.instagram.com/paolamoon.cuantica?igshid=OGQ5ZDc2ODk2ZA==
https://www.glamaestheticsgroup.co.uk/

I think that every day, needs arise that motivate many people to start new ventures and you should not be the exception. We know it can be intimidating, but if you hold on to a source of inspiration it will be amazing to see the happiness of seeing your achievements realized. For this reason I have dedicated a large part of my life to founding small and medium-sized businesses in the health and well-being sector in search of optimizing health from the integration of body and spirit.

MEMORIES OF A TRAVELER

By Paola Montes

That which is firmly established on the mental level is destined to emerge eventually in reality...

I was just a teenager, full of unanswered questions, trying to find the path that would lead me to a future full of love and freedom. The only thing that was clear in my mind was the feeling of wanting to be an entrepreneur, to focus on a sector that I was passionate about and that would allow me to grow financially and mentally.

At home, I had as an example a strong, intelligent, and determined entrepreneurial woman: my mother Jimena, who *has been* a most *important* support for the development of many aspects of my life. Also, my *recently deceased* father Diego *Antonio who* was an inspiring man, a frame of reference in our city for his solidarity and support to the development and growth of our city *and the region*. He was a loving, cheerful, and dedicated father to my brother Diego Fernando and me *and a loving grandfather to our children.*

We have had the support of these wonderful people giving their best as parents as well as our grandmother Luisa *Albina*, a loving and invaluable pillar in our entire family. To them I extend my *measureless gratitude.*

On the way to destiny we are co-creators of our own destiny and this is something we experience on a daily basis.

I started a magazine and an agency of public joyful events while studying for my degree in Social Communication at the Universidad Autónoma de Santiago de Cali, Colombia. I started in the trade alongside my best friend, with whom I battled hard to carry out the first issue of the magazine that was distributed for free in the main cities of Colombia.

We started together from the visualization process, and that was the way the first popular concert organized by us for a fair in Cali was born. We dreamed of what it would be like to fill a stadium and present the artists that we, as part of an audience, would like to see. That is how we started from the approach and visualization without underestimating the importance of strategic work and discipline. I think it is important to start a project from within, to connect that energy with God and the universe, from that creative energy that will help you to empower and orchestrate every step you take.

Luck favors the prepared mind because he who teaches himself perceives opportunities better, and the world calls that *'luck'*.

I faithfully believe that education opens countless doors. And I do not believe that knowledge comes only from an educational classroom; complementary with it, it is of great value to educate ourselves in topics or sectors that bring value to our lives and nourish it with diverse teachings.

We must be ambitious and greedy for our own mental and spiritual self-improvement.

In search of new opportunities and experiences, *with the support and love of my dear husband,* I decided to embark on my journey to a charming city, London, which not only opened its doors to me in a warm and welcoming way, but was also the place that opened another aspect of my life as a mother of our three children: Mia, Samuel and Joseph, charming creatures that have added to bless my passage through this world.

My initial goal was to continue specializing in advertising and marketing but since I suffer from dyslexia and it is difficult for me to pronounce a number of words accurately, I was not accepted into the Department of Social Communication at London Metropolitan

University. It was a difficult time, although now in retrospect, I know that other opportunities were being orchestrated at the same time for me - I just had to be ready to receive them.

Every time we are faced with a "No!" or whenever a door closes on us, we empower a fear that paralyzes us and drains our energies, as if wanting to take us down a path of defeat and depression. We have all at some point experienced that feeling of rejection, whether it comes from a client, a boss, an institution, or even a romantic relationship. The point here is not how the situation presents itself, but rather how we can turn that outcome, that decision, in our favor. We have the power to create wonderful things for our lives no matter where we start and how many times we have to start over.

As Sad Guru puts it, *"The wisdom of life is that whatever life throws at you, you can also make something wonderful out of it"* ...

I decided to apply to university again, this time using my technical knowledge in nursing, my other passion. I thought that if what I needed was to improve my English, what better way to do it than at the university and at the same time get another university degree? As it's said in my country, killing two birds with one stone. I received my offer at the London Metropolitan University for Human Nutrition and Dietetics. So, full of illusion and pregnant with my third child, I started this beautiful career.

Everything requires effort and a strategy to help you reach your goal. In my case meditation was one of the most important weapons to recharge my energy, dedicating the first 20 minutes of my mornings to thank and connect with the Creator was and is fundamental to my personal, spiritual, and financial growth. In my meditation after thanking for my life and those of my family's, I let go of all kinds of problems, difficulties, illnesses, and everything that represents a burden for me and I give it to Him, to that God or universe that has unlimited answers and I rest in Him. Another important step in my meditation is part of the co-creation or visualization, giving me the privilege of submerging myself spiritually in that sea of possibilities and vibrating high with the strongest. With the door that I want to be opened, with that result that I long for, embracing it as if it were already done and again giving thanks and being full of joy, I am ready to start a new day.

The world is your materialized state of consciousness. It is tremendously faithful and reflects what you have created. In the middle of my university career, I was worried about how to continue generating income for myself and my family without having to interrupt my studies and without completely sacrificing the free time I had for my little ones. I had to leave aside the feeling of panic from not having a clear picture and get rid of any sense of lack since I did not have a large capital at that precise moment of my life to start a business.

I decided to connect with my inner self, and from a state of meditation I decided to start attracting business opportunities to my life. I chose to smile every time the problem came to my mind instead of getting stuck in asking, "How will I do it? What company I can create with little capital and still think about the little time I would have left to devote to the project alongside university and the children?"

It was a situation that, without good emotional management, would have easily confined me in a depression or fed the opinion of dropping out of college and looking for a conventional job. It was time to decide, and not precisely because I had many opportunities at that precise moment, on my attitude to face the situation. Whether I would be willing to give that extra mile of effort in waiting without neglecting my college work and as a mother and wife without losing focus of the desire to form my company, without lowering my guard to take that opportunity, recognize it, and take it. So, day after day, I decided not only to believe in myself and in my potential as a professional but also to believe that every time I was getting closer to that door that would open for me, of that opportunity that was already brewing from the creative energy.

¡When the answer comes from the least expected place!

Thinking about my parent's stable situation, I thought of taking a family loan as an approach to starting my business in the UK. But at the least expected moment, my family fell victim to the political situation in my country. At that time, Colombia was going through one of the strongest waves of violence and my parents had been victims of violence by the Colombian guerrillas in the Pacific area. Being banished from their hacienda and losing their crops and cattle ranching business, they were forced into exile because their well-being and lives were in danger.

After this misfortune, they fortunately relocated to other cities and had the political support of a government program that, although not restoring what was lost financially and emotionally, provided them with the protection to be safe outside the country.

When the situation could not be more tense, one of my colleagues at the university brought to the table a business plan to start a clinic of aesthetics and preventive medicine, having as an investor Angel - one of his brothers. That's how we opened our first location on Harley Street in the heart of London. Thanks to our professional skills and the technology that we implemented in our clinics, we were able to position ourselves favorably in the market. Every step is important; not everyone has the same pace, it can be one brick at a time, but you must make sure that you are not static, and that no situation, no matter how difficult it may be, can paralyze you. And if it is the case that your body is limited in movement, you have the most powerful weapon to create 'your mind'.

"When you change your inner self, you begin to see the changes happening on the outside. You stop being the victim in your life and become the creator of your life" (Dr. Joe Dispenza.)

After completing my studies as a dietitian, I am dedicated to promoting preventive health. Our company faithfully believes in the connection between body, mind, and soul or energy and that as integral beings, we must take care and encourage not only good feeding but also the balance and strengthening of our mind.

Another part of my time is dedicated to cultivating these same seeds that my parents left implanted in me - determination, gratitude, passion for what I undertake, and above all love for my children.

Back to my homeland.

Returning, enjoying again the fresh breezes of my beautiful Valle del Cauca. My family once again started in the field of crops and livestock. When a passion is so great, no matter how many obstacles are in your way, tenacity and love for what you do will give you enough energy to achieve it. Now we are three generations enjoying these beautiful landscapes, and the smiles of my children get lost among the songs of the various birds of the region. Amid family warmth, mountains, bonfires, and good wine, I witness that we have the responsibility to draw a future worthy of our lives.

Lastly, here are my tips to embrace self-love while working in the wellness[1] industry which are essential for your own well-being and effectiveness in helping others. These are some steps to help you cultivate self-love in your professional life:

Understand Self-Love: Start by gaining a clear understanding of what self-love means. Self-love is about accepting and nurturing yourself and others, recognizing your worth, and treating yourself with kindness and compassion.

---

[1] *The Global Wellness Institute defines wellness as the active pursuit of activities, choices and lifestyles that lead to a state of holistic health.*

Set Boundaries: In the wellness industry, it's easy to become overwhelmed with helping others and neglecting your own needs. Set clear boundaries to protect your time and energy. This may involve scheduling breaks, limiting work hours, and saying no when necessary.

Practice Self-Care: Prioritize self-care as an essential part of your daily routine. Engage in activities that nourish your body, mind, and soul such as exercise, meditation, reading, or spending time with loved ones that make you happy.

Continuous Learning: Stay informed about the latest developments in the wellness industry. This not only benefits your clients but also boosts your self-confidence and self-worth while setting you apart in your field.

Self-Compassion: Be kind to yourself when you make mistakes or encounter challenges. Remember that no one is perfect, and self-compassion is an integral part of self-love.

Regular Reflection: Take time to reflect on your own wellness journey. I always keep a journal. It helps to understand your own triggers, challenges, and personal growth areas. This self-awareness can help you relate better to your clients.

Seek Support: Nobody is perfect. Don't hesitate to seek support from colleagues, mentors, or therapists if needed. Sometimes, talking to someone who understands your industry can provide valuable insights and emotional support.

Celebrate Achievements: Acknowledge your accomplishments and milestones, no matter how small they may seem. Celebrating your successes reinforces a positive self-image and it keeps you motivated.

Mindful Communication: Be mindful of your self-talk and the language you use when addressing yourself. Replace self-criticism with self-encouragement and positive affirmations.

Disconnect When Necessary: In a digitally connected world, it's easy to be on call 24/7. Learn to disconnect from work when you need personal time and relaxation. This is key to me to connect with my family and little ones.

Build a Supportive Community: I Surround myself with like-minded individuals who understand and appreciate the importance of self-love and self-care in the wellness industry. This serves me well to establish great partnerships that lead to more businesses and friendships that keep me nourished.

Regular Self-Reflection: Dedicate time for self-reflection and journaling. This can help you process your thoughts, emotions, and experiences, leading to personal growth and self-discovery.

Share Your Journey: If you feel comfortable, consider sharing your own wellness journey with your clients. This vulnerability can create a stronger connection and inspire them on their own paths to self-love.

Remember that self-love is an ongoing journey, and it's perfectly normal to have ups and downs like I did throughout my life. But by prioritizing self-love and self-care, you'll not only enhance your well-being but also become a more effective and empathetic wellness professional. Your personal growth and self-love will also serve as a source of inspiration and motivation for your clients and allow you to connect on a deeper level.

Try this and if you have any questions, suggestions, or comments), please contact me.

Instagram: Paola Montes @paolamoon.cuantica
@glamaestheticsgroup

Paula Arredondo

Co-founder of The Face Workout S.L.

https://www.linkedin.com/in/paulaarredondo/
https://www.facebook.com/TheFaceWorkoutOfficial/
https://www.instagram.com/thefaceworkout/
https://www.thefaceworkout.com

Urbanite, endlessly cheerful, Paula Arredondo boasts 22+ years of experience in consulting, management, and R&D project development. A law graduate, she honed her marketing and communication skills in the vibrant city of London.

There she discovered her passion for promoting health and personal well-being, which has been the primary focus of her professional journey in recent years.

Back in 2013, she blazed a trail as a pioneer in using Instagram for business and digital marketing methodologies, enabling brands to propel their projects showcasing their values and reputation.

Her thirst for knowledge keeps her at the forefront of innovative resources related to physical health and emotional balance, making her a walking encyclopedia in these fields.

With an unwavering passion for everything she undertakes, Paula thrives on forging connections between ideas and people. This passion culminated in her latest venture, The Face Workout, Spain's inaugural facial gymnastics brand, where she is Co-Founder.

THE WELL AGEING RESEARCHER

By Paula Arredondo

"People think self-care that it's all about self but it's actually taking care of oneself so that we can show up better for everybody else. More energy more capacity, more stain power (...) So it's really refilling the fuel tank in my mind as opposed to the kind of egocentric narcissistic that a lot of people take" —Andrew Huberman

About me

Even beginning to describe myself is the hardest thing there is! Creative, independent, courageous, determined…

There is always one description of oneself that is the light and another much darker one, one that we don't even want to recognize ourselves.

For many years, well into my adulthood, I thought I had a happy childhood - a model, in fact. Not only did I think so, I felt happy for many years. However, it's true that I suffered from unhealthy shyness and that there were certain things that I simply didn't dare to do. I was super critical of my image to the point of falling into bulimia.

Reality was not the rosy color I wanted to see everything in.

So, life took me, or rather I took my life, through many places from my native Santander to Madrid, Algeciras, Tarifa, and back to Madrid. I would not say it was a straightforward path, but I would say that my curiosity for other experiences and my desire to improve myself made me overcome challenges and reach my goals.

And now I'm sitting here writing to tell you how all these achievements, this search for more and for perfection that never arrived led me to a search for love for myself. This is the story I come to tell you today, as well as the people who have helped me to love myself and to take care of myself more than ever.

My way of loving myself is a journey. It is a process of discovery, curiosity, and pampering.

I think the first time I started to think something was not right was when I lived alone for the first time. I would wake up many times at night in a panic with the certainty that there was someone in my room watching me. That anguish had lived with me since I was a child. I would wake up, knowing that I was at home with my parents, my family... whoever it was. I would calm down by myself until I went back to sleep. When I started living alone in my minuscule attic in Madrid, there was no one to protect me.

So I began to ask myself, why do I have these panics that are so frequent?

These panics were compounded by the fact that for the first time in my adult life, I didn't have a partner. I was looking for a partner but the men I was attracted to were emotionally unavailable. The pattern repeated itself over and over again. Realizing this put me on alert but I still didn't really realize what was going on. It was just an awakening.

There were pieces of the puzzle missing. I had to go to London to do the hardest thing I have ever done in my life: learn English at the age of 36, leaving behind a career as a consultant in R&D projects to start from scratch. Six months with neck pain, not being able to speak, and completely losing my personality and identity by not being able to express myself in the language I knew until then. A lot of studying and the discipline that I apply when I am motivated to achieve something pays off.

This is really the beginning of a love story, the most beautiful one I can tell - the love story with myself.

Until I achieved this challenge, perfectionism had prevented me from enjoying the many accomplishments I had achieved until then. Law

Degree. Studying for a Master's Degree in the European Union and finding a job in a small consulting firm right after finishing. Setting up on my own. Getting a job at the Autonomous University of Madrid as a manager of R&D projects in applied mathematics... I saw it all as a matter of luck (and in part it was, I kid myself not) but I failed to see that I was the one who had sought and brought about that luck.

I didn't feel as if I had fully owned my achievement until I got my B2 in English. The five years I lived in London were some of the happiest of my life.

So, with that English that opened the doors to so much knowledge and so many new relationships, with that achievement that I felt was my own and not a matter of chance... Chance itself put me in contact with the people and techniques that have brought me to where I am.

Michelle Lowbridege. The Energy Editor

It is no coincidence that my professional career has always been linked to research. I have a curious mind and an infectious disposition to spread the good things I discover to share them with the people I love and who are close to me.

I came into contact with the work of Michelle Lowbridge, *The Energy Editor,* in 2014 by chance on Facebook. It offered some free "energy" editions, although I don't quite remember what they consisted of. Her proposal has always been linked to the identification of fears, thoughts, feelings, and limiting beliefs that prevent us from achieving the things we want.

I would never have approached her work if she had done it in Spanish. Only a language new to me, free of the cultural baggage that many of the words and ideas she discussed, allowed me to be curious about her work and try it out in my energy field.

And what power it had. How I regret not following her mandatory care to the letter. So I began to work with her on editing (and eliminating) a number of fears she had identified. Then, I worked on thoughts, limiting beliefs, and more through each new course she offered online.

Her work is simple to apply. Through kinesiology, she identifies the words or phrases that need to be edited from a person's energy field. The position of the hands and the repetition and feeling of that word or phrase for a certain time helps to release the blockage. And that's it. Then follow the self-care rigorously so that there are no unpleasant consequences in its release.

Here is the link to her courses:
https://www.michellelowbridge.com/valuable

At that time my life was in chaos. I had returned to Spain to be near my sick father and things were not easy.

Thanks to Michelle and a group of light healers she invited me to join, I met my second teacher: Amanda Foy. Michelle introduced her to me to help my father with his illness. Needless to say, my loving father thanked me for my interest but said no way was he going to work with her.

Amanda Foy. The Emotional Strength Trainer.

The traumas or emotions that we do not process make us sick, besides making us very sad...

I came in contact with Amanda through my father. I met her thanks to a marketing strategy project and only later got to know her work thanks to her program to heal affective relationships.

That was intense. Not only because I became aware of many dynamics that I had witnessed in my family and that began to make sense of many things. But also, thanks to this work, I discovered something that

I had intuited for years and that gave the explanation to my night terrors of years ago.

I discovered that I had been sexually abused when I was very young. Different events made the pieces fit together. This knowledge has triggered many others.

Without wanting to go into details that have no place in this chapter, this discovery was the point of no return. It was the tip of the iceberg really, but it became a very firm place to keep working on.

Amanda is one of the funniest and most caring people I know. Her sense of humor and laughter is infectious and her work is incredibly delicate and precise.

For years, I was part of her weekly healing program where each week she removes a thin layer of the onion we have built around ourselves for protection.

In addition, I had the opportunity to attend one of her retreats in Fiji, a life-changing experience, as well as taking me and my soul sister to the other side of the world. I will never be able to express in words the deep gratitude I feel for that trip, for that experience.

Amanda's work focuses on identifying and clearing the traumas she sees in your energetic field with an incredible ability to identify them and with a scientific approach that also led me to her.

https://amandafoy.com.au/ and her people

The English language removed the cultural burden of certain words and methods that I would not have approached had it been in Spanish. However, my logical mind has always searched for explanations.

Woo-woo and its scientific treatment

Given my experience in R&D work, the search for the scientific explanation of why these things work I have discovered in the book

Why Woo-woo Works by David R. Hamilton, Ph.D. of which I incorporate here an excerpt from its introduction and which I recommend to all those interested in the subject.

"The Oxford University Press's definition of woo-woo is 'Unconventional beliefs regarded as having little or no scientific basis, especially those relating to spirituality, mysticism, or alternative medicine. The term is believed to have been coined in the 1980s, possibly in imitation of the wailing sound associated with ghosts and the supernatural.

Many complementary therapies, healing modalities, treatments, and other practices, theories, and beliefs are often referred to as woo-woo, but this is because they're not widely understood and most people are unaware that in some instances, they've a sound basis in science."

This book addresses different scientific studies' topics such as the placebo effect, "energy healing" and finally telepathy, distant healing, and prayer.

I was already devoted to these tools because they have worked for me, but I believe that this approach from a more scientific point of view can help many people.

Audrey Jeanneau and chiropractic

Working with my emotions was on the right track. I had done therapy and had my two supports. Then, I discovered that eliminating blockages in the spine and nervous system also had an effect on my emotional well-being.

This was taught to me by Audrey, and chiropractic practices have been a part of my life since I met her over three years ago. With her knowledge of chiropractic and kinesiology, she has helped me to find that balance.

Our nervous system controls and coordinates all the functions of our body from the brain to each of our organs, cells, muscles, and tissues. If the nervous system is functioning properly, our health is optimal.

With the accumulation of physical, emotional, mental, chemical, and electromagnetic stress, the spine becomes blocked and interferes with the nervous system. Chiropractic releases the spinal blockages to allow optimal functioning of the nervous system and ensure wellness at all levels.

More than nine years of working with emotions, of looking inward, of wondering what is wrong with me, of seeing how I fell again and again in the same place, of bad digestion, of the inability to do 10 sit-ups in a row have become a place of possibilities, of a curiosity that opens to the path of abundance.

Paula Echeverri. NeuroMomCEO

Whatever happens is convenient, and the timing is always perfect.

So, when I met Paula Echeverri, we immediately saw the possibility of working together. I have been very interested in breathing and meditation for years and have tried many things, but working with her was different because of the order and depth she has given to her NeuroFit program.

Working on resilience is essential for our lives because life is going to pass us by faster every day. With breathing techniques and meditations completed with my all-time favorite app, I have felt more optimistic and relaxed no matter what life put in front of me. It's been a long time since I've felt this way and it's amazing.

Her work is based on neuroscience and other, more holistic techniques, focusing on helping us process the emotions that overwhelm us. Whether it's an anxious, depressive, or hopeless state, she teaches you how to move to another state where you feel more creative, optimistic, and calm. This is accomplished through techniques that, once learned, can easily be practiced at your own pace, when you need it.

Definitely the cherry on top of my self-care. I am happy and recommend it to everyone I see who is having difficulty processing their emotions.

The longevity path or giving life to the years with The Face Workout

This search for wellness and balance has led me to connect with my life path. Another pillar of longevity and happiness in life. This has led me to The Face Workout, a project that began as a spin-off within a beauty center and has become the first brand to offer facial gymnastics in armchairs in Spain.

Our proposal is based on the premise that if training our body has such good results, not only physical but also mental, why have we never been told that we could also train our face?

So, together with expert facialists, luxury organic cosmetics, and the latest in facial appliances, we have created a series of workouts to receive in an armchair that your face trainer will perform after having asked him/her about your facial fitness goals. You are then recommended exercises and self-massages to do at home as well as tools and protocols.

In a social and cultural moment where we are obsessed with beauty, with staying always young, with the dysmorphia of the filters of platforms and social networks, this proposal of facial exercise to harmonize and give health to your face is completely innovative. We want to take away the power of anti-aging and the messages of fear and limiting thoughts that pervade culturally and instead give it to well-aging. To know that we can do many things to have better facial health and be noticed.

Our mission is to revolutionize the promotion and encouragement of facial well-aging through non-invasive techniques, treatments, and products. Making it accessible to everyone, by time, price, and location. Because we know that the best face is the one that is trained.

This mission has given me the opportunity to continue researching and advancing on how to promote longevity. How to love ourselves more and to be happier.

There are a few solid pillars to support well-aging:

- Sleep more than 7-8 hours a day.
- Eat little and of essential nutrients, incorporating intermittent fasting if possible.
- Doing sports, incorporating strength and endurance exercises.
- Having good mental health: being able to regulate emotions.
- Having a good social life: key to longevity.

From The Face Workout, we explore each of them to make it accessible to our community, with the focus always on facial gymnastics.

Now, when I looked back, I couldn't help but feel a sense of fulfillment. My journey as a wellness researcher has taken me to places I had never imagined, both within myself and across the world. With each experiment and experience, I was one step closer to unraveling the secrets of holistic well-being. The next chapter of my journey awaits promising new challenges, discoveries, and, above all, a profound sense of purpose in my quest for wellness and self-love.

In gratitude and dedicated to the memory of my father Juan Manuel Arredondo, who taught me so much and was as curious as I am in this search. Thanks Dad.

Divya Chandegra

Founder of Chit Ltd

https://www.linkedin.com/in/divyachandegra/
https://www.facebook.com/Life-and-Wellness-with-Divya-115873590689176
https://www.instagram.com/divya.chandegra/
https://www.divya-chandegra.com/
https://www.divya-chandegra.com/subscribe

Divya Chandegra is the Founder of Chit Ltd, which stands for 'Consciousness' in Sanskrit. A certified yoga teacher, reiki practitioner, author and wellness soul guide, her mission in life is to empower parents and professionals to heal their subconscious limiting beliefs and blocks to free themselves and future generations from repeating patterns that keep them trapped in cycles, through conscious decision-making and conscious living.

Divya is passionate about guiding others to heal unconscious behaviour patterns to avoid passing unidentified blocks onto future generations.

After spending almost two decades in the creative technology sector in a self-sacrificing mindset and an imbalanced vibration of over-giving, people-pleasing and constantly needing to do and be better, Divya discovered the path to true fulfilment.

For free wellness tips and access to her Unblock Your Self masterclass to begin your transformation journey today, sign up on her site: www.divya-chandegra.com/subscribe

NURTURING SELF-LOVE BY RELEASING THE CONDITIONS OF CULTURAL EXPECTATIONS

By Divya Chandegra

The past

I wasn't always like this… I was invisibly anxious, lacked genuine confidence, and didn't understand my worth or my value. And because of this, I was constantly chasing – looking outside of my Self for gratification and validation. I was chasing – through my career, through my need to be right, through my need to be 'perfect' in the eyes of others – whilst at the same time wanting to defy all of the cultural, societal, traditional programs, and gender stereotypes instilled in me from childhood that didn't feel true to my Soul.

My anxiety was invisible to the world. And that in itself took a lot of energy and effort. I showed up for others because I never had anyone consistently show up for me when I was a child. I offered words of positive affirmation and acts of kindness because as a child, that's what I was desperately seeking and all I really needed to make me feel accepted and loved unconditionally.

I grew up in a strict, traditional Indian family. My parents were trying to retain their traditions and culture and my siblings and I were part of the first-born British-Indian generation. This lifetime has allowed me to span two centuries and five generations of our lineage. I had a lot to contend with in terms of expectations and obligations and I was carrying generational wounds without even realizing it…

Get an education, but be subservient to men.

Get an education, but get married as soon as you get your degree.

Get good grades in your education, but attend 1000 extracurriculars, community functions on weekends, host guests at the house multiple nights a week, learn to cook and clean, speak only when spoken to, make food for your brothers who are studying for their exams, and clean your brother's room *and* the whole house. Are you stupid? Are you deaf? Get out of my sight...

Get married and then have kids, but get it *all* right the first time, because failure is unacceptable.

It's no wonder that one of my fears was the inability to breathe.

We didn't know how to talk to each other in our household - to express ourselves, be affectionate with each other, or even be kind to each other. I didn't know what love was. The relationship model I witnessed as a child worked for them, but for me, it was broken and I've spent decades figuring that out and rebuilding my belief systems to know that I can now create my own template, despite what society and my culture expect.

It's hard when it's something you want to believe in so much and when it's the people you love. Facing a reality that you choose to break free from can awaken something deep in your Soul. And, only in facing the upsets, can I *really* be free in my heart and Soul – because I'm being true to my Self, knowing that what worked for them won't *ever* work for me, because I know my Self now, I love my Self now. Instead of following what others expect of me, I'm following my own path. I'll start from scratch if I have to, and I've really had to.

The present – is a constant and active practice

I've created and am giving you my top 11 tips for learning how to truly love your Self - things that I've had to break down and rebuild on my journey to self-love. I have faith in you and trust you'll find something useful for your journey here:

1. **Building a relationship with your Self** – is a priority. We put a lot of effort into building connections and giving to others, often at the expense of spending that time and energy on better learning about ourselves and identifying our own needs. More often than not, it's because we're looking to others to fulfil our unmet needs. When we redirect that focus, attention, and energy inward, we learn to give to ourselves instead of expecting from others. Fulfilling our own needs first allows us to build the connections outside of ourselves from a place of fullness instead of want and need. Check in with your Self daily and ask, 'What do I need right now?' And then give that to your Self.

   Top tip: It could be something you need to do for your body (movement, massage), something to stimulate your mind (reading, learning), something to calm your mind (meditating), or something for your emotional well-being (meeting friends, affection). Your needs on any given day will be unique to you and your lifestyle, and making it a practice to check in with your Self empowers you with the awareness of your ability to take care of your needs.

2. **Discovering your values and principles** – can change your life. We're raised with the values, principles, and belief systems of our parents, role models, and caregivers in childhood and we move through life unconsciously without questioning whether these remain true to us as adults. Your experiences will lead you to have different values and principles from your parents and you have the ability to reprogram your belief systems and to sit down and question what *your* values and principles really are, so giving your Self the time to prioritise this task is important.

Top tip: I've learned that some of my values and principles are my unmet needs from childhood e.g. trustworthiness, non-judgement, compassion, consistency, and reliability.

3. **Finding your creative expression** – is a way to bring balance to your being. In life, some groups in society value creativity, whilst others view creative expression – quite frankly – not as a way to build a career. Everyone needs a form of creative expression. It harmonises the logical and creative parts of the brain. So, while your creativity may not be directly linked to your career, it could be something that brings you joy. Have you tried experimenting with drawing, painting, dancing, cooking, acting, learning a musical instrument, or even writing? I find writing gives me the ability to express my thoughts and feelings (something I struggled with in childhood) and it comes naturally to me.

   Top tip: You don't need to make a career out of it (although you might), but it should be something that makes you feel free and brings you joy and may be seen as a form of releasing stored energy from your emotional, mental, and physical body.

4. **Developing your self-awareness** – relates to building a connection with your Self. More than just identifying your needs and giving to your Self, self-awareness is about understanding your behaviour patterns, your reactions, how you talk to your Self and others, keeping your Self accountable, and taking conscious and intentional action to maintain, evolve, or change the patterns that are keeping you trapped in unwanted cycles. Doing this incrementally and with compassion and kindness for your Self allows you to accept and heal and to come to others with an awareness and understanding of where *they* are in their journey.

Top tip: Recognising patterns in your Self, is also about acknowledging the wonderful and beautiful qualities you have and being kind to your Self.

5. **Reframing perceived failures** – as lessons and experiences you had to go through to learn and evolve is a reprogramming exercise. In childhood, you may have been criticised or taught that 'failure' is unacceptable in life. We're taught that 'failure' is a negative experience, but that's someone else's thought or opinion. This puts a lot of pressure on a child and on your inner child as an adult. The truth is, if we don't fail, it means we're never learning, and I'd rather fail and learn a thousand times than never do or try anything because of a subconscious fear of failure. Give your Self the grace and permission of the learning curve when experimenting with new or unknown experiences – that's what living is all about!

    Top tip: You can choose the experiences you want to have, so why not choose to live and keep learning?

6. **Accepting to forgive your Self** – is a great place to get started on your self-love journey. We're often tough on ourselves because *we* put pressure on ourselves or because we feel pressured by societal and familial expectations. We have to release these expectations and accept where we are in our journey. If we remain stuck in the energy of an inability to meet false expectations, this leads to resentment and this energy can build up and keep us stagnant because we're constantly, subconsciously blaming ourselves for not achieving, or worse – reinforcing that we're not good enough.

    Top tip: To get to forgiveness of your Self or of others, you have to get to acceptance, so let's start being real and compassionate instead of wearing false masks because of external expectations.

7. **Developing Self-trust** – is a key aspect of your relationship with your Self. It can carry you through any challenges you may face and drive you to conquer any obstacles that come your way when striving to achieve your goals so that you can begin to thrive! Self-trust allows you to show up for your Self so that you're not depending on or relying on others to show up for you or holding others to *your* expectations. It brings you freedom and independence, even when moments of doubt arise.

   Top tip: Demonstrating to your Self that you will consistently do what you say you're going to do builds discipline, reliability, and consistency, and in the long term rewires your subconscious to believe that you've got this – whatever 'this' is!

8. **Exploring your emotions** – will quite literally set you free. We're led to believe that our emotions are fixed and the negative experiences of these emotions block us from releasing and overcoming them because we don't want to face them. What if you explored one emotion at a time to understand where it comes from, how it impacts you as an adult, and how to release it or treasure it with love?

   Top tip: I learned how to build a relationship with two emotions, namely resentment and loneliness. Identifying that they exist in the first place was a major task (as I was never allowed to express, explore, or understand them as a child), and then replacing the negative connotation with acceptance and understanding allowed me to transmute the trapped energy I'd been holding on to for decades.

9. **Learning to let go** - of things, people, and energies that no longer serve you with love and gratitude is a skill. It's liberating and calming for the nervous system and relates to surrendering

the things that are beyond our control so that we can use our energy on things that we can change within ourselves. Ultimately, it's about trusting and having faith that what's meant for you will not pass you by, whichever path you take to get there. It enhances the trust you have in your higher Self and the Universe so that you can free your energetic field and the blocks in your body to be open to receive.

Top tip: Practice breathwork and meditation by activating and engaging your senses to bring you to the present moment. This also helps as a technique to ease anxiety.

10. **Learning to set healthy boundaries** – is essential for self-love. It can be challenging if you were raised in an environment where giving outside of yourself was valued more than giving to your Self, or the way others viewed you was prioritised over how you viewed your Self. If you find it challenging to say 'no' to others, then you're likely to find it a challenge to set healthy boundaries.

Top tip: You can only really set healthy boundaries when you've built a connection with your Self and have established an understanding of your own needs.

11. **Practice gratitude daily** - to shape the way you start or end your day. Being grateful for the smallest things elevates your vibration and frequency. Love is the highest frequency.

Top tip: Practice these as affirmations or write them down where you can see them to recite them daily.

I'm grateful for…

- the air that I breathe
- the water that cleanses, purifies, and heals my energetic field

- my mind, my body, my cells
- the earth that grounds me, supports me, and allows me to realise my goals and dreams
- the drive and passion within me to achieve them
- the sounds of the birds
- the sweetness of the air
- this food that nourishes and sustains me
- the warm touch of a loved one
- my ability to see the good in everything
- my ability to set boundaries to protect my wellbeing

As adults, we get to decide how we show up for ourselves today, the examples we set for future generations, and the roles we consciously (or unconsciously) play in their lives. Will you choose to lead by example – by learning to explore and heal your own wounds, limiting beliefs and false programming? How can we ever love someone else when we haven't discovered what we need to heal in order to love ourselves fully and completely? Our connections can only be based on superficialities, expectations, obligations, needs, and wants rather than complete acceptance, understanding, compassion, and freedom when we haven't done the work to achieve self-love.

The ongoing journey

"The only way to unconditional love (for Self and others), is through self-love" – Divya Chandegra

Identifying and unearthing all of the upsets, fears, and subconscious programs from our childhood that impact us today requires care, consideration, patience, and compassion. Remember to be gentle and giving to your Self as you begin to create a different, wholesome connection with your Soul Self. Only when you learn to love your Self truly and deeply will you be able to open your Self up to experiencing *real* and true connections with others.

The ability to experience, be, and resonate with the frequency of unconditional love - for yourself and others - begins with learning to love your Self unconditionally first.

To get you started on your journey to self-love, check out my eBook, *Success Starts with Self: 35 Must-Read Articles to Set You Up for Long-Term Success* focusing on Wellness & Self-Care, Connection & Relationships, Success & Growth. It's available to purchase on my website for immediate download: www.divya-chandegra.com/books

You can also subscribe for free holistic wellness tips and access to my Unblock your Self masterclass and Understanding your Inner Child mini-lesson at: www.divya-chandegra.com/subscribe

Lyn Lozano Galicia

CEO of Barcelona Ideal Services

https://www.linkedin.com/in/lyn-lozano-galicia-/
https://www.facebook.com/BCNIdealServices
https://www.instagram.com/lyn.lozano.galicia/
https://www.bcnidealservices.com/

Lyn was born to her humble parents in the South Eastern part of Luzon in The Philippines, moved to the beautiful city of Barcelona over a decade ago looking for a new blueprint for the future. Back in the Philippines, Lyn has experience as a prototype/project technician in a multinational-level company in the engineering department.

Being strong-willed, persistent, unstoppable and with tons of ideas in mind, she started to develop a skillset to make it happen.

Incessant hunger for learning, excellent communication skills, natural leader, with strong social conscience, an imaginative problem solver who exudes natural confidence.

Lyn is professional with a decade of experience catering to International clients, founded the company in mission to help expat community and locals alike to make their life easier by providing ideal services such as nannies, babysitters and housekeepers and more. Being in the business gives her the opportunity to augment her experience not just for herself but to clients and staff too. It is serving fellow humans that gives her satisfaction and fulfillment. Rendering service this way can be repaid by seeing happy and appreciative clients, which goes beyond the monetary compensation that comes with it.

A JOURNEY OF RESILIENCE AND SELF-LOVE AS AN EXPAT

By Lyn Lozano Galicia

As I gazed out of my window, my thoughts drifted back to the Philippines, the place I had once called home. It had been several years since I had made the bold decision to leave my native land and embark on a journey to Spain. I have come a long way since then, both geographically and emotionally.

When people think of moving to a new country, they panic, but I knew there was more to me than what I found in the Philippines where I grew up. I love my culture but I was yearning to have new adventures, excitement, and to learn about new cultures. I think my confidence and self-love helped me so much. I always had big dreams and goals that I needed to explore.

I am a people person. To be honest, sitting here alone in my apartment in Barcelona is too much for me as I enjoy sharing and connecting with people with similar interests and creating new opportunities for my business. I am able to connect easily and bring many good things to others. However, it was not as easy as it looked.

I had always been a dreamer. I had a vision of a life that transcended the limitations of my small hometown. The bustling cityscape and the diversity of cultures have always fascinated me. In the Philippines, I worked in a multinational company in the engineering department but my dream was to become a renowned massage therapist, one who could help people find relaxation and relief from the stresses of their daily lives.

The Philippines was the starting point in my career, but I knew that my dreams would take me far beyond its borders.

The decision to leave my family, friends, and church where I was involved in children's ministry at the time was not an easy one, but it was a necessary step on my journey to success. I loved my family dearly and missed my two nephews and niece, Luc, Lee, and Kaixin. But I had to follow my intuition, so I took a leap of faith.

I arrived in Barcelona with a bag full of hope and determination, not knowing anyone in the city and with a basic understanding of the Spanish language. The first few months were tough. I took up a humble job to make ends meet.

The challenges I faced were daunting; I learned the Spanish language and I made a home in the expat community in Spain. I learned that my resilience was unwavering. I immersed myself in the culture, made expat friends, and gradually honed my skills. I also pursued my passion for massage therapy by enrolling in a reputable training program.

My first job was as a nanny and as a massage therapist at a small wellness center tucked away in the heart of Barcelona. It was here that my journey truly began to take shape. My clients, a mix of locals and expats, soon discovered that I had an exceptional talent and natural charm. I have a gift for making people feel at ease and cared for, and my massages were nothing short of extraordinary.

Besides my career, I had to do some coaching and self-work to learn that I was holding onto things that were not good for my future. I had to let go, and that was not easy. I worked hard under those limitations and freed myself. Now I am happier than ever.

I am so grateful that my business spread like wildfire about the Filipino massage therapist who had a magical touch. Soon, my appointment book was filled weeks in advance. It wasn't just the technique; it was the genuine warmth and kindness that I used that kept my clients coming back. I had an uncanny ability to connect with people, understand their unique needs, and tailor my massage accordingly.

Customer service is a tough thing to do when you are a service provider but my patience and attention to detail were the best and people really love that.

My reputation grew, and with it came opportunities. I was invited to work at high-end spas, resorts, and even for Barcelona's elite. Yet, I remained humble and dedicated to my craft. I knew that success was not about just making a name for myself; it was about helping others find peace and relaxation, and that is something that moves me and fills my heart to help others find what they need with my help.

After years of hard work and saving, I started a company that provided services to others like a nanny, massage, house cleaning, and others. My dream finally became a reality. I opened my business "BCN Ideal Services" in Barcelona focusing on English-speaking customers who needed help with many things. I ventured, and it was the best decision I made. I am not afraid of trying new things. It keeps me engaged and motivated when days are hard. I learned that if I let things flow they will come my way and that my will and mindset are unbreakable, even in the hardest times when I was doubting myself thinking, "Did I make the right move?" I always get the best out of myself when I go and disconnect in nature. Feeling the beauty of it makes my heart whisper its wisdom, and then I can make a decision easily.

My success was not just about the massages; it was about the overall experience. People at the time in the middle of the COVID-19 pandemic trusted me and my skills to make them feel calm and taken care of.

I also believe in great leadership which I studied here in Barcelona at a university. Leading with care is important and I have instilled in my staff the same commitment to exceptional customer service, kindness, and genuine care that I have always practiced. Clients left not just relaxed but also with a smile on their faces, eager to call again and share their wonderful experiences with friends and family.

I also began offering specialized services for expats, understanding the unique stresses and needs they faced. My business became a home away from home for many, a place where they could find solace and comfort in a foreign land just like I did.

I think going for the expat market was key to my growth as an expat myself. I knew all the problems and hurdles of moving to a foreign country and I translated that into my business and the experience people get all the time. My advice is, if you ever think of making a move, remember always that "home is where your heart is". Mine is now here in Barcelona where I created mine after a lot of work and tears.

Here are four tips for a woman who becomes an expatriate in a new country:

Research and Prepare:

Before moving to a new country, it's crucial to research and prepare thoroughly. Understand the local culture, customs, and laws, especially those that may impact women. Learn about the healthcare system, transportation, and any safety concerns. The more you know in advance, the better equipped you'll be to adapt to your new environment.

Build a Support Network:

Expatriate life can be challenging, and having a support network is essential. Connect with other expats, both women and men, through online forums, social media groups, or local expat organizations. Building a support system can help you navigate the challenges of living in a new country, share experiences, and provide a sense of community.

Safety and Cultural Awareness:

Safety should be a top priority. Familiarize yourself with the local safety guidelines, emergency numbers, and any specific precautions you should take as a woman in your new country. Additionally, be culturally aware and respectful of local customs, dress codes, and social norms to help you integrate smoothly and avoid any misunderstandings.

Pursue Your Interests and Hobbies:

Moving to a new country is an opportunity for personal growth and exploration. Pursue your interests and hobbies, whether it's joining local clubs, taking up a new sport, or participating in cultural activities. Engaging in activities you enjoy can help you meet people, find a sense of belonging, and create a fulfilling life in your new home.

Remember that adapting to a new country takes time, and it's okay to seek support and guidance along the way. Embrace the adventure, stay open-minded, and be patient with yourself as you navigate this exciting chapter in your life as an expatriate.

In my journey, I learned that it is important to give back. I empower my Filipino community and others through my services and I find it important as a woman of faith. I never forgot my roots, or my religious beliefs and I used my success to support causes close to my heart. I sponsored scholarships for young Filipinos looking to pursue careers they like to be. I also supported charity events to raise funds for local and global causes, earning a special place in the hearts of both my clients and the community.

Faith definitely has a place in my heart and I find it a great way to connect with universal love and my self-love practices. Keeping your faith can be important for self-love for several reasons, although it's important to note that the role of faith in self-love can vary greatly depending on an individual's personal beliefs and values. Here are some reasons why faith can be significant in fostering self-love:

Positive Self-Image:

Faith can provide a framework for believing in your worth and inherent goodness. Many religious and spiritual traditions teach that every individual is created in the image of a divine being and has intrinsic value. This belief can promote positive self-image and self-acceptance.

Forgiveness:

Faith often encourages forgiveness, both of oneself and others. When you have faith, you may be more inclined to forgive yourself for past mistakes and shortcomings, which is essential for self-love. Letting go of guilt and self-criticism can lead to a healthier relationship with oneself.

Hope and Resilience:

Faith can provide a sense of hope and purpose, which can be crucial for self-love during challenging times. Believing in a higher power or a greater purpose can help you navigate difficult circumstances and maintain a sense of resilience.

Community and Support:

Many faith communities provide a sense of belonging and support. Being part of such a community can help combat feelings of isolation and loneliness, contributing to improved self-esteem and self-love.

Guidance and Values:

Faith often offers moral and ethical guidelines that can help individuals make choices aligned with their values. Living per one's values can boost self-esteem and self-love by promoting a sense of integrity and authenticity.

Mindfulness and Inner Peace:

Some faith traditions incorporate practices such as prayer, meditation, or mindfulness into their teachings, which can help individuals connect with their inner selves and find inner peace. These practices can be instrumental in self-love by promoting self-awareness and self-acceptance.

Purpose and Meaning:

Faith can provide a sense of purpose and meaning in life, which is closely tied to self-love. When you feel that your life has a purpose and your actions are meaningful, it can enhance your sense of self-worth and love for yourself.

In my case, I enjoy going to my church and feeling the vast power of their words filling my heart and soul. It helps me to keep motivated in everything I do.

I believe in the power of living intentionally as a woman, which involves consciously making choices and taking actions that align with your values, goals, and desires. It's about living a purpose-driven life and being true to yourself. Here are some steps to help you live intentionally as a woman that I learned from my journey:

Self-Reflection:

Take time to reflect on your values, beliefs, and what truly matters to you as an individual.

Consider your long-term goals and aspirations, both personally and professionally.

Identify any areas of your life where you feel unfulfilled or disconnected from your true self.

Set Clear Goals:

Define specific, achievable goals that align with your values and reflect your aspirations.

Break these goals down into smaller, actionable steps to make them more manageable.

Regularly review and adjust your goals as needed to stay on track.

Prioritize Self-Care:

Make self-care a priority in your daily routine. This includes physical, emotional, and mental well-being.

Set boundaries to protect your time and energy. Learn to say no when necessary.

Practice mindfulness and relaxation techniques to manage stress and maintain balance.

Embrace Your Identity:

Celebrate your identity as a woman and embrace all aspects of it.

Be confident in your choices, whether they involve career, family, relationships, or personal growth.

Surround yourself with supportive and empowering individuals who respect your identity and choices.

Seek Personal Growth:

Continuously seek opportunities for personal growth and self-improvement.

Challenge yourself to learn new skills, explore new interests, and expand your horizons.

Be open to feedback and constructive criticism to help you evolve and grow.

Cultivate Healthy Relationships:

Build and nurture positive relationships with friends, family, and partners.

Surround yourself with people who uplift and support you in your journey.

Communicate openly and honestly in your relationships to ensure mutual understanding and respect.

Advocate for Yourself:

Be an advocate for your own needs, rights, and aspirations.

Stand up for what you believe in and work towards creating a world that aligns with your values.

Support causes and organizations that promote gender equality and women's rights.

Financial Independence:

Strive for financial independence and security to have greater control over your life choices.

Manage your finances wisely, budget, and save for the future.

Invest in your education and career development to increase your earning potential.

Lead by Example:

Serve as a role model for other women by living authentically and intentionally.

Support and mentor other women in their journeys towards self-discovery and empowerment.

Practice Gratitude:

Cultivate a mindset of gratitude by acknowledging and appreciating the positive aspects of your life.

Regularly reflect on your achievements and the progress you've made on your intentional living journey.

The key is to learn from those experiences and continue to grow and evolve as a person. Your journey as a woman is unique, and living intentionally allows you to create a life that is true to yourself and your aspirations.

My journey from the Philippines to Spain was filled with challenges, from being alone to not finding my true calling, but it was also a journey of self-discovery and triumph and I would not change a thing.

Everything set the stage to meet the people who surround me today. I am grateful every day for everything I get, and when I am down I rely on God and a friend who can listen and give me some tough love when it's time to make an important decision.

I have turned my dream into a reality, and in doing so, have touched the lives of countless others, proving that no dream is too big to achieve with determination, perseverance, and a heart full of compassion.

Rebecca Ann Hemmings

Dr Rebecca Ann

PhD

https://www.linkedin.com/in/rebecca-ann-hemmings-23924136/
https://www.facebook.com/rebeccaanntherapies
https://www.instagram.com/rebecca_ann_therapies/
https://www.drrebeccaann.com/

Rebecca is a Ph.D. in Natural Medicine, a Mama, and since 2007 a Business owner. In 2012, Rebecca began specialising in working with people to harmonise the Body, Mind, Spirit, and Soul into alignment on the premise of Quantum Physics, Energy Medicine, and Neuroscience to activate people's innate ability and drive for health and healing. Rebecca supports people to overcome Stress, Anxiety, Depression, CPTSD, Trauma, Overwhelm, Burnout, and Chronic Illness, by optimising mental and physical health. Rebecca's fusion of knowledge and her own experiences with chronic illness, along with genuine care for others shapes her unique multidimensional approach to health through empowering people.

FINDING THE HERO AND HEALER WITHIN

By Rebecca Ann Hemmings

"Letting go of who you think you are supposed to be and embracing who you are." —Brene Brown

The unraveling and releasing of pain is what allows us to truly emerge with self-love.

Self-kindness goes beyond how we treat ourselves consciously; it penetrates every level of our multidimensional being.

As I lay feeling helpless, wondering why this is happening again - every muscle in my body clamping, the longest continual seizure, 30 minutes of pain in my body, confusion in my mind, jaw clamping, whole body trembling - I finally hear 'her'. She is the fearful voice inside of me, the aspect of me I had denied and rejected. She was screaming "Stop it, stop it, STOP IT." I responded to her, to my whole body and being with, "It's ok, you're going to be ok." I repeated this phrase over and over to myself for the duration of the seizure. That simple act of kindness directed towards myself in that challenging moment changed everything for me. The seizures no longer consumed or gripped my life, in fact, they slowly disappeared altogether.

I realised I had been preaching self-kindness for years with my clients and only now, in one of my darkest moments, was I able to consciously connect with that wounded part of myself that was simply afraid. The seizures had triggered that part of me that didn't like pain, that did not like uncertainty. My traumatised inner children were undeniably having a hard time accepting this medical situation. Even the medical community had no understanding or answers. The uncertainty knocked me off balance and pulled the rug from under my feet. Resistance only exacerbated the symptoms; acceptance has a funny way of unravelling. Like a gaseous substance when it's compressed it can become volatile, but when given space it simply disperses. Unresolved emotions within me were making the whole experience even more icky and unwanted.

Let me give you a bit of background: I attended a very mild and conscious plant medicine ceremony (San Pedro) on the day of that particular seizure. I asked the medicine to show me the way to peace and acceptance for all that I had been experiencing since having COVID-19, and subsequent persistent COVID symptoms for years afterward. Effectively this was a combination of all the work I had done leading up to this particular seizure. It took me a while to even say the word 'seizure' out loud or even tell anyone. I felt confused and embarrassed. When I couldn't walk for days afterwards due to muscle fatigue from the clamping, and my partner would carry me to the bathroom, I would say to myself, "It won't happen again, this is the last time." Looking back now I realise I was in denial, ashamed, and confused. Therapy helped me be able to accept what was still happening.

After this superficial level of acceptance, I did two EEGs that showed abnormal, electrical brain activity in the left lobe. I had always wanted to do an EEG ever since I studied brain mapping and neurofeedback with Dr. Joe Dispenza at Quantum University. The doctor I had was extremely unsympathetic, shouting at me to stop jerking and ticking, the nurse snapping back at him, "She can't help it", as they flashed a strobe light into my eyes and had me hyperventilate for long lengths of time. I am not epileptic and that's all they wanted to confirm. One of the many medical doctors I passed through in my two-year post-COVID journey mentioned it may have been a stroke in the brain during the infection stage. At the initial infection stage, I was admitted to the hospital twice and given oxygen and intravenous paracetamol to try and break my 40°C fever that lasted weeks. Each time I was released as I didn't meet the requirements to stay hospitalized during that time. I didn't have pneumonia, my lungs were fine. Meanwhile, this virus was busy attacking the rest of my body, and brain, and deepening into my central nervous system.

I hoped it would end, along with all the other evolving and all-encompassing symptoms such as:

- Neurological issues - some loss of movement/speech
- Memory loss
- Chills and tremors
- Seizures
- Nausea
- Widespread body pain
- Gastrointestinal pain
- Confusion, feeling lost, scrambling to think
- Loss of sequences
- Air hunger
- Irritability
- Fatigue (myalgia and malaise)
- Tachycardia
- Dyspnoea
- Heavy and painful muscles
- Extreme hair loss (telogen effluvium)
- Headache (extreme pressure behind the eyes)
- Extreme thirst and dehydration
- Sensory sensitivity (noise/light/scent)
- Parosmia - changes in taste and smell (chemical scents/smoke stuck in my head giving me a headache for weeks at a time, the smell of most things has changed forever for me)
- Anxiety and depression

- Shingles three times in one year after COVID - my immune system was flawed

The irony was that when I got the initial infection in July 2021 I was already pretty overwhelmed. The previous year was the breakdown of my longest relationship which was with my business partner, and I was a new mama. I had also spent long hours on the phone with the consultant as my dad was in the Intensive Care Unit with COVID. My auntie also passed away quickly after contracting it. I still believe there is a genetic component to this infection, but I'm also a powerful believer in epigenetics and the environment determining which genes are active. So, after nursing my partner and son with COVID at home, of course, I got it whilst wearing a neckbrace from an old injury flare-up, with a UTI infection, and taking antibiotics, and cramming to complete my Ph.D. defense paper. My defenses were certainly not optimal! In hindsight, I wish I had given myself the grace and the self-kindness to rest more. Nevertheless, within a few days, I was already overwhelmed by the virus itself.

According to a <u>study</u> published in January 2023, at least 65 million people worldwide have been reported to be suffering with Long Haul COVID (PASC), accompanied by over 200 symptoms across multi-organ systems being reported. It appears many people experience overlapping and evolving symptoms over time, which can be confusing and frustrating when you're looking for support. Even people who experienced a mild case of the infection were found to develop Long COVID. <u>The 12 symptoms that studies</u> most set apart for those with Long COVID are: post-exertional malaise, fatigue, brain fog, dizziness, gastrointestinal symptoms, heart palpitations, issues with sexual desire or capacity, loss of smell or taste, thirst, chronic cough, chest pain, and abnormal movements.

This was the inspirational quote I used whilst writing my Ph.D. defense paper. It's quite prophetic as the following years were some of the toughest and self-enlightening.

"When heaven is about to confer a great responsibility on any man, it will exercise his mind with suffering, subject his sinews and bones to hard work, expose his body to hunger, put him to poverty, place obstacles in the paths of his deeds, so as to stimulate his mind, harden his nature, and improve wherever he is incompetent" –MENG TZU

The undeniable truth was that I had this realization midway through my six-year journey to completing my Ph.D., but was wisely convinced by my mentors to keep going. But after I had completed the work, it hit me like a ton of bricks. I had been doing all of this to feel worthy, just to feel some sense of being good enough, some approval, and self-worth. Was it necessary? No; I clearly didn't need to put myself through all of that only to realize at the end that I felt the least accomplished and worthy I could have imagined. I had subconsciously put so much meaning into that effort, the disappointment of that self-realisation mixed with Long Covid, and the death of my little Pepe, my 13-year-old French bulldog who was my closest companion, which all happened within the same period of summer 2021. Would I do it again? Yes, simply because I love the subject of Quantum Health - I love learning! My Human Design profile is 1/3, this profile typically has a deep need to explore and learn from direct experience. I am a natural-born researcher. I had been doing it all my life without even realizing it.

I clearly remember being eight years old in a neck brace (no one knew what happened to me - probably tension), watching the Barcelona Olympics, considering my next move because nobody wanted me; I was being kicked out of home, my mum was not stable enough yet to take me in, and my grandad said I couldn't live with him. In my eight-year-old mind, I felt alone and rejected. I stared at Freddy Mercury and Montserrat Caballé singing operatically "Barcelonaaaaaaaa" at the

1992 Olympics on my TV screen, projecting myself there. Only when I was 28 years old and living in Montjuic where the Olympics were held, walking my dog around the stadiums where Freddy Mercury had sung all those years ago did I realize that I had shifted quantumly. Yes, it had taken a few years, 15 to be precise, to get here but I made it. I'm here! Even without conscious intention, our subconscious may be working on an intention or belief that we had many years ago.

In my childhood, I experienced emotional and physical abuse and neglect. I had CPTSD and without realizing it at the time, those adverse experiences were shaping me, and unfortunately dysregulating my central nervous system. Luckily for me, I was also extremely determined. Even though I was often undermined, I knew I would overcome the challenges and blaze a new path for myself and my life. And I did, leaving England in 2007 to settle in Barcelona and become a business owner at 23 years old. Although living in my dream city, doing my dream job of organizing events, and working for myself, I was still on my journey of self-discovery and healing. I spent my first five years in Barcelona under the watchful eye of my extremely toxic, criminal, gangster boyfriend and his entourage - think W   olf of Wall Street. The lifestyle was intense and driven by money, drinking, and drugs. I knew I had to escape him and finally, with enough courage after a particularly violent attack, I left him and never looked back. Throughout the whole relationship, I kept squashing that inner compassionate self, my intuition, whatever you want to call it that kept telling me "This will never work out, leave now!" It got to the point where I could no longer ignore that voice. My physical and mental health was on the line yet again and it was time to move on.

That same voice reappeared; like a classic codependent, I switched one for another and got myself into handing my power off to my newly found Guru from India who stayed at my home and turned it into an Ashram in 2012 and 2013. As you may have noticed, things generally happen all at once, at least with me they do. And so one month after leaving my toxic romantic relationship, I had an accident on my Vespa. A car with a trailer overtook me on a turn and swung into the back of my elbow. My arm turned limp and green immediately, so I shouted "Help me!" while still sitting on my moped, not realizing the damage. Fueled by adrenaline and the need to get back to my dogs after being at work all day, I actually tried to walk home until a kind stranger on his cigarette break from working at Burger King put his arm around me and I collapsed instantly. I guess my nervous system needed a signal to stop. I woke up in the ambulance, and then without any pain relief my wrist was pulled to pieces in Accidents and Emergencies where the bones became even more shattered. They put me in a cast and sent me on my way saying it would be fine. There was that inner voice again, niggling at me that something was not right here. So I persisted with the doctors in my broken Spanish. Not being heard, I turned to more private doctors who discovered through an MRI that things were definitely not going to heal without intervention. Some bones were even facing the wrong way. My wrist was completely shattered and I needed emergency surgery the following morning to have a new metal wrist. The doctor told me I would have lost my hand altogether if I'd just left the cast to heal the bones that were all deformed. I'm so glad I challenged what had been repeated to me by my doctors!

Ok, so back to the Guru (monk). After my accident and learning to be ok being alone, I begged for a sign and quickly was introduced to Swamiji. Firstly, I did learn a lot; the meditation and calm were very useful and I'm grateful for all I learned through that experience. But there it was again, that voice, this time even in my dreams. That's the voice of intuition, my very own self-kindness, and it told me my Guru had intentions for sexual relations; I even had dreams he was chasing me to rape me. In true toxic, spiritual community style, I was told these intuitions were just my own impurities and to address my own bad thoughts myself. I was being gaslit! Unfortunately, it came to light that there were sexual relations happening in secret between the monks and disciples, again validating that part of me that felt something was not right. This was an abuse of power; young women were being preyed on. Well, that was a wild ride into my thirties and that's just the condensed version. All of this reinforced to me that I should listen to the intuitive voice within me and become that self. It had my best interests at heart. That's where I have an abundance of self-kindness I can access anytime I need. Learning to love myself, be kind and gentle, and listen to my loving internal voice was a healing journey.

Whilst having Long COVID I remember being interviewed by Masks For America and asking them to change a line that read, "This is a chronic illness Rebecca will never recover from," referring to the chronic fatigue and fibromyalgia the doctors had told me I now likely have. They quipped back with a Mayo Clinic link to say how these conditions are incurable. I replied very seriously that I would recover and I knew my body was phenomenal, and where I am now, with all the love and acceptance, I know I will get better.

Luckily for me, I had 10 years of holistic health experience in my toolbox, but of course, I still had a whole lot more to learn. Firstly, regulating my maladapted nervous system. The resource of simply having faith in myself and my healing process, knowing the quantum possibilities of healing after achieving my Master's and Ph.D. in Quantum Medicine, I was really being tested to put it into action.

The following therapeutic approaches are what I used to support me on my healing journey.

Recovery has been processed in stages of healing; please note that healing is unique to you and certain therapeutic approaches may be healing in certain stages and not applicable in others.

I really believe you should listen to your own body - your body is phenomenal, and you know yourself better than anyone, better than even medical professionals. Developing the ability to listen to my body and articulate my needs has been one of the most instrumental tools in my recovery.

- Pacing
- Gut microbiome testing and targeted support
- Biohacking
- Nervous System Regulation
- Art therapy to draw me before, during, and after seizures
- Red Light Therapy
- Quantum Inner Child Healing
- Chiropractor gentle and specific
- Acupuncture
- Massage
- Quantum Healing
- Vagus Nerve Stimulation
- Autophagy at the right stage of healing
- Eating clean
- Eliminating chemicals
- Self-kindness
- Understanding my personality type and how that may become energy depleting

It was not one incident that led to my getting sick; it was the culmination of many things coming together like a perfect storm. COVID was the straw that broke the camel's back. I needed to address every aspect to find my roadmap to healing.

Self-kindness was particularly important when I was stuck in bed in a dark room, fatigued, and unable to move for days at a time. These crashes were frequent and debilitating. Being such an active person all my life, I felt inadequate and like a bad mother. One day my two-year-old son had an accident but I was unable to move to take off his clothes. He asked me for food, but I was pinned to the bed. Staring at my hand, willing it to move. It took me 20 minutes but eventually, I was able to get him a tangerine and then collapse back down. It was hard to have self-kindness in those moments. I felt ashamed and afraid. That was the part of myself I finally met during the seizure - my healer and hero, self-kindness, my own self-love.

This whole process has deepened my awareness and compassion for all people with chronic illnesses, autoimmune diseases, neglected people suffering in silence, those feeling burnt out or unsupported by the medical community, or those feeling that pharmacological solutions are not always the only path to healing or suitable. I realized there were so many people forgotten, gaslit, or ignored by the medical community for decades. I hope that the silver lining in the disaster that was the COVID-19 pandemic will produce more funding and research into chronic illnesses.

The importance of self-kindness when you're going through something challenging like an illness is a tremendous source of strength. Accessing that divine essence is your superpower. I always tell my clients their higher self is basically their compassionate self, that is the part of you that is unconditionally kind to yourself even when you are suffering, even when you feel like there's no way out of a situation. You still love yourself.

What I've learned so far along my journey is not only to listen to that inner self-kindness, but also to let go of control and embrace and love the authentic version of myself, not the idealized version but the one I am in this moment. I champion her.

Lottie Heffer

Founder of Surrender To The Breath

https://www.facebook.com/surrendertothebreath
https://www.instagram.com/surrendertothebreath
https://www.surrendertothebreath.com

Lottie Heffer (B.A, PG Dip) is trained in Integral Breath Therapy (Master level trainer and facilitator), Trauma Informed Somatics and Expressive Arts Therapy, and Art Therapy. Lottie provides certification training programs and workshops in Integral Breath Therapy and works with clients in personalised sessions in Barcelona and Online.

Her workshops include interactive and educational sessions on emotional regulation and resourcing with a strong focus on somatics and art therapy. She is coordinator and facilitator of Poiesis EXAT Online, a 50hr online program delivering trauma resources to healthcare professionals, specifically in situations of crisis, pandemic, loss and trauma.

Lottie is an advocate for grief work and founder of How's Your Mourning? (2020), a free weekly online support group available to anyone going through bereavement. You can find out more about her and her work here: www.surrendertothebreath.com

BREATHING BACK TO LIFE

By Lottie Heffer

Grief. You don't know it until you're there, right in the middle of it all.

My personal healing journey began over 15 years ago. I had left the country I had emigrated to along with the relationship that had taken me there. I didn't understand or know at the time that loss and grief could be attributed to more than the death of a loved one, and that the loss of a home, country, job, relationship, or even pet, can open up old wounds of past grief. I had no awareness to give myself space to feel. I was very much a "pull your socks up and keep going" type - being born into the Keep Calm and Carry On dictates of post-war Britain, still very much present in UK culture, didn't help. But, something told me I needed to ask for guidance in processing this really icky, uncomfortable feeling and incredible heaviness and sadness. That was my first experience of therapy, and there began my journey into psychology and psychotherapy.

I find the mechanics of the mind fascinating and felt very safe and contained in these first CBT therapy sessions. I became so interested that I moved to Barcelona in 2010 to study and qualify for a post-grad in Fine Art and Art Therapy. I've always been an artist, and now finally I was studying psychology through my own medium. I loved it. I loved the creation process and the symbology. I had not made the connection between mind, body, emotion, and spirit at the time. I was, intuitively, creating art that was serving a therapeutic purpose for me. Now, when I look back at the art I created, it speaks volumes to me, the voice of the subconscious is definitely evident. The themes that I was unconsciously exploring are themes I work with consciously today.

Our subconscious minds are very clever, they lead us to our healing. Mine led me to a career of teaching art to kids for six years. It couldn't have been better for my inner child - the creativity, fun, joy, and play. Alongside this, I was nurturing my adult life, creating beautiful jewelry pieces, and delving into the body with physical exercise and then yoga.

However, it was during this time away, that my sister was diagnosed with Cancer, and within weeks, my mum. My sister thankfully caught it early, but Mum was a different story - stage four progressive with a mastectomy. I don't know how, but she managed to make the journey lighthearted. Mum was a big boobed lady, one down and waiting for constructive surgery she would joke about being lopsided and what kind of nipple tattoos she was going to get. Things felt ok, normal. It didn't feel like she was going to die.

But my life did start to change behind the smiles. It kind of leaked out. I was four years into Barcelona and with the man I had met when I had first arrived. His family had become mine, and I felt like I was living in a Woody Allen movie. But our relationship started to fall apart, and after some long painful months finally ended. I threw myself into everything the way I knew how, by doing. Doing yoga, doing exercise, doing work…My flatmate called me a machine, a title I was proud of.

I dived into an Ashtanga Yoga Teacher Training, attracted to it for its routine and unforgiving almost military approach to the practice. I learned the hard way. I gained an injury and collapsed into burnout from pushing too hard and fast. I distinctly remember rolling my eyes when it was suggested that the severe vice-like headaches and fainting spells I'd been having could be connected to stress. I just didn't see how that could be possible; I felt fine after all, so how could it be?

By the summer of 2015, I was a mess. I seemed fine on the outside, holding down two great businesses, teaching yoga on the side, and renovating my home…. but I was also going out every night, coming home with strangers, drinking until I couldn't feel, getting in at the early hours of the morning, going to work sick and bleary, and repeating it the next day.

At one point, I asked my ex-boyfriend to come and take away all the alcohol bottles from my house and hide them, because I couldn't do it anymore. He did. It lasted about a month until my Dad came to stay and I couldn't tell him I wasn't drinking because I felt so ashamed. So I started again.

I was trying to prove to myself that I could do it. That I was strong, successful, and had it all worked out. I needed to be perfect; the vegan, non-drinking, lotus-sitting yogi, otherwise, I felt like a fraud.

I knew all the theories, but I didn't apply them to myself. I signed up for therapy and saw a wonderful Gestalt therapist for four years, who is now a colleague of mine. And slowly, very slowly, things started to drop into place and a wider understanding of how we are interrelated first within ourselves, and then with others began to grow and transform.

She showed me acknowledgement, and forgiveness, and provided a safe space to explore thoughts and emotions. She also held space for me to come to the understanding and acknowledgment of the depression, abandonment issues, self-harming, drinking, sexual promiscuity, and damage I was doing to myself and my body and to seek help for it. This was the first key piece in my healing and planted a seed.

I hiked the North Camino De Santiago from start to finish. I had read the book Wild and got inspired; I figured if it worked for Cheryl Strayed it could work for me. It turned out that a miracle fix wasn't my answer. I walked for 5 weeks and felt great, and two weeks after returning home, I sank back into a deeper depression. It took a lot of courage, and a lot of talking with my therapist, but I finally opened to the idea of antidepressants.

We cannot heal anything if we can't see it, and acknowledge it's there. I knew everything on an intellectual level, I had studied, but I didn't attribute it to ME. I thought the word "trauma" was overly dramatic and something Americans use (sorry any of you Americans reading this, please forgive me). My therapist had suggested AA a couple of times and I batted the idea away, saying I was fine; after all, I wasn't waking up to drink whisky from under my bed. And honestly the word alcoholic was definitely not a word I wanted anything to do with. I dismissed all of it, but it stayed at the back of my mind and I'd ponder over it occasionally.

Anyone who has been a part of the Yoga community or AA will have probably experienced many conversations around taking pills as an escape, as a cop-out. That it can all be worked through, that you're just not trying *hard enough*. Anyone feeling like that, please come and talk to me. YOU are perfect the way you are, there is absolutely nothing wrong with you. Anyone who shames you for owning up to owning what you need and relinquishing the constant fight needs to understand the effect their opinions and words can have on another human being.

Very slowly, I started to feel better. And then my mum got sick again. It was 2016, the summer; I was whining myself off the antidepressants and had come home to spend the summer with Mum to do so. It was beautiful and relaxed and fun. That Christmas, she got diagnosed with Cancer the second time around, the terminal kind. It was a week after her own twin brother had lost his wife. I remember thinking it's time to be strong, for her.

I know what it feels like to experience grief.

We made the most of the time we had. Mum was in denial and saying she was going to live for years, which I found frustrating and painful as it closed off any processing or grieving together of what was happening.

In November 2017, my beautiful granny got pneumonia and passed away. She was the matriarch of the family, this incredible jolly wonderfully smiley woman. I had to leave her two days before she passed, it was heart wrenching to leave and get on that plane. It was a fairytale death if there is such a thing. She was 96, everything was perfect. What it didn't do was prepare me for what was coming.

At the exact time she died, I was actually meeting an old friend, Gabriel. I felt like he was a gift, I called him Angel Gabriel. He was someone I had met seven years previously in Mexico volunteering. We started a very intense, trans-Atlantic relationship filled with promises and hope. I really believed this was it. He moved to Spain. The same month, Mum got really sick.

It was impossible to do both, but I tried. Here was this man that had arrived from across the world to be with me, and my mum, in England dying. Mum and I were so close that we had one of those almost telepathic relationships. Every time she went into hospital it was like I knew and had booked my flight home to be there with her before she had told me. I tried to nurture my mum and my new relationship and failed miserably at both. I didn't know how to ask for help. I broke up with my boyfriend, and on the same day, hours later, I got a phone call from my stepdad saying this was it, the hospital had said we needed to come.

I know what it's like to go from being the daughter to caretaker to seeing the look of pain and confusion on your mother's face. The last two weeks everything happened so fast and at the same time in such a daze. Mum didn't know what was happening. They said there was nothing more that they could do. We took her home to be comfortable. We didn't know at the time but we only had 10 days. On her last night with us, I asked Hoo my step dad if I could sleep in the room with her. When mum passed away early the following morning Hoo, my sister and I were there holding her hand as she took her last breath.

I didn't cry at the funeral. We got the train back to my dad's house that night. I didn't know what to do with myself. I felt so lost. I desperately wanted someone to take the reins of my life and tell me what to do. Me and Gabe flew back to Spain two weeks later. It was my best friend's 40th and I wanted to be there for her, and everyone was throwing her a surprise. I was in a daze and not able to make logical decisions. Gabe promised me he would stay in Spain with me and we would work something out, I didn't know what else to do, my life was there. We got on the plane. The next day, the day before her birthday, Gabe told me he had booked a flight back to the States and was leaving the next day.

The day he left I put my dress on, painted my face, masked up, and performed like I knew how. I could get an Oscar for my performance that day. It wasn't until four months later that I finally collapsed.

My world came crumbling down.

It brought me to my knees. I hid in my little flat in the centre of Barcelona and just cried. I shut everyone out because I didn't know how to be in public and feel that much pain. The mask had finally fallen.

I hid where I could be raw and real and feel in the only place I knew, alone. Some people were so amazing at that time who held my hand through that process, not the people I expected to be there. They often say that about death; the ones that show up are hardly ever the ones you think. They were brave. I was angry and irritable.

Irritability is a symptom of depression, and depression is so often unexpressed anger turned in on itself. I wouldn't let myself express anything; I was so afraid of my anger, of hurting someone, anyone, and that they too would leave.

Everything stopped. All creativity stopped. The only thing I could do was cook, read, and sleep.

They diagnosed me with Complex Grief and PTSD, attachment, abandonment, and dysfunctional emotional regulation. My grief opened up old wounds, and all my resources were gone. A system that had been a survival mechanism that I had devised and put in place early on as a small child had come crashing down and was not working anymore. I didn't know which way was up. I'd find myself on the kitchen floor in my flat holding onto the tiles with my palms, sobbing and shaking, feeling as if I was going to fall. I had never heard the sounds that came out of me before - animal, primal screams. I was terrified.

I stopped drinking because it didn't work anymore, it just made everything more painful. There was no escape from this deep loss I was feeling. I started going to AA but felt so confused. I had made my mum my rock, my God, even though I was 36 at the time. I missed her so much I couldn't go forward. Everyone else went about as if nothing had happened, going out for drinks, smiling, laughing. I just wanted the world to stop.

I felt like I was going crazy.

Our own family fell apart and everyone went into their corners. I tried to get people together for a bit, but then I just couldn't do it anymore. I had to heal myself. My head was filled with my partner who had left, with desperation, deep raw grief, and pain. I remember feeling that I was worthless, that I had to be such a bad person for someone to leave after my own mum had died. Nothing made sense to me.

I had hit rock bottom. And I'm so grateful. (you might hate me for saying this and I get it, I mentally spat at people when they said how grateful they were and I was in the deepest of pain). I had no choice but to let go.

"The cure for pain is in the pain." —Rumi

Not unlike the situation we found ourselves in not so long ago of lockdown and uncertainty, there was no escape. There was nowhere to run and hide and avoid, so I had to stop. And listen. And feel. Sitting with emotion. Sitting in the unpleasantness of it all. In the dirt, in the muck. Being present. Because with grief there is nowhere to run. It is all-consuming.

I knew I needed to face my pain and feel it. For me, that looked like:

Firstly, quitting alcohol, so I could feel. I wanted to feel everything. I didn't want to numb any of it anymore.

Secondly, community and support. I knew I could not go through this grief alone and that it wasn't good to isolate, even though that was exactly what I wanted to do. I flew back to England to be with family for a month and to go to grief support there, but it was full of older people who had lost their partners. They were lovely and welcoming, but there was no one of my age or circumstance there. So, when I felt able enough, I set up my own. More importantly, I joined AA, which gave me daily meetings and a place to sit in community.

And *thirdly,* I knew that I needed to go beyond the words. I had muted myself. I felt deep knowing that I needed to be in my body. I needed to express my anger and deep sadness. I needed to find a way out of this big, perspex box I felt trapped in.

A friend came for tea and told me two very important things. The first was, "Your mum has just died, it's ok to cry." On hearing it I felt this huge wave of tears pour out of me. I was so afraid of crying because I didn't know when or if it would stop. She invited me to put a fence around it, to contain it, like putting a fence around a big park so that kids can ride their bicycles round and round freely in safety. The image still sticks in my mind and is something I use today. I felt relief for being given the ***permission to feel.*** From that point on I dropped into my body and felt everything. And I haven't stopped.

The second thing she told me has been one of the most determining things I've done and has played a major, life-changing role. She told me about a breath training that was taking place in the States in Florida. Sometimes we have wise friends, and we listen to what they say because we know they speak the truth. This was one of those moments. She had shared Breathwork with me previously and we had done some sessions over the years, perhaps four or five, and so I understood and experienced the power and potency of this work. Still, I have no idea what I was in for with a group session. She had trained many years before in Israel with Carol Lampman, and she invited me to look at a training that was coming up with her in the next few months. I signed up.

While I waited for the training to come, I went fully into my body. I took shiatsu massages which opened floodgates, I went to a beautiful week-long grief retreat where I experienced community, sharing, and being seen and heard and celebrated, in all my feelings and expressions, for the first time. I realized this was what I wanted to do. I wanted to support people in their grief. I wanted others to experience this, to know that they can feel in community, that they are worthy, too. That they matter. To be seen and heard, and witnessed, in their pain while receiving support, love, and nurturing. That it is ok to express yourself.

I came home and explored Expressive Arts Therapy, this time as a client. I wanted to see if what I believed in and studied really did help people with trauma and loss. I went to see a Body Psychotherapist who specializes in Rechian techniques and stayed with him for over a year. What I was doing was learning to be in community. Learning to express and be in my body, in a group. I still didn't speak. But I was moving, feeling, being.

When the breathwork training came, I was so terrified I almost didn't get on the plane. The process had already begun. Carol is an incredible being with a fountain of knowledge and over 35 years of experience in this field. In those six days, I laughed, I cried, I met some incredible people, and I felt a deep knowing and understanding that this was it. On the first day she recollected a story of her training with her teacher: "What's the fast track?" His reply was simple: "You're on it."

That first day she passed a microphone around and we had to introduce ourselves. For someone who has spent a lifetime hiding behind shame, this was possibly the worst thing that could happen. Not ONLY was I going to be seen, but HEARD as well? Oh crikey. But I did it, and what I learned from this beautiful community of people, on the other side of the world to my home, was that I belonged. Carol was so wonderfully amazing at creating this beautiful cocoon of a space, **where we all heard each other. Where we all saw each other. And in witnessing someone else's pain, a healing began, collectively.**

Something that I had been interested in studying and reading about, I was experiencing and feeling for the first time. I could FEEL what it was like to slowly gain trust and to open up and how this reflected. I could feel unconditional love. I went back to certify as an Integral Breath Therapy facilitator and to train in level two, advanced IBT, and Masters Level. Now I have the absolute honour of training others in this work. Sometimes I still have to pinch myself.

One myth I want to set straight right now is that the journey is never over. There is no endpoint. Others may have had their miracle moment, and that's wonderful. Mine has been a succession of little moments, little unsure steps towards something, not knowing where you are heading. The journey is part of life; we are constantly learning, growing, and evolving.

I have found, however, a deep, knowing of myself. A profound understanding and acceptance. An empathy and compassion towards myself. I've felt held and safe in spaces that gave me permission to express and release my anger, judgment, fear, and most importantly for me, my shame. The more I continue to investigate and explore, to learn to love and accept myself, I have found that I don't react so much to others' opinions of me or opinions of them because I'm ok with myself. What **I've found is that in being ok with myself, in all my humanness and mistakes and choices, in all my aliveness and awkwardness,** I have become much more open to receiving the people around me in their aliveness, in their choices, and their expressions.

I want other people to feel what I felt. I want other people to know they can courageously face their pain. I want people to experience being in their bodies and what is underneath fear because it is the most beautiful bliss I have ever experienced.

Breathwork delves deep into your being; it unearths you, whatever is in there, it will bring it up for you to experience, acknowledge, and release. After all the intellectualization, I got to feel. By making the unconscious conscious, we have the ability and awareness to create change. In the lifting of denial and acknowledgment of those hidden feelings, pain, beliefs, and trauma, we have the opportunity for healing.

You cannot heal what you cannot feel.

First, we need to bring awareness, because how can we address something if we don't know it's there?

It takes courage to dig deep, but when we do, it's worth it. Underneath anger is often fear, under fear is deep sadness, and under the sadness, is the unconditional love that we all have. By releasing our emotional, physical, and mental blocks we free up space for the free-flowing being that we are, for Eros, for vitality.

When we speak our shame, we help and encourage others to do the same and to heal. To open up to acceptance. To love.

I have found Expressive Arts Therapy to complement breathwork in such a beautiful way. It has allowed me vital and crucial integration.

Creativity and play are so important to our healing, they are the opposite of danger. What we are really doing is finding pockets of safety, pockets of connection.

What I have found important is not the continual scratching away at what is wrong or finding proof to feel shame that will reinforce our core beliefs of "I'm not good enough," or "I don't belong". Instead, seize the opportunity and space to be witnessed in community, in gentle holding, in a relationship. This acknowledgment and celebration of who you are. We are creators. We came here to create. So I invite you to ask yourself; What do you want to create in this world? What do you want to fully live, to let in, to feel, and to experience? Because it is all here for you.

Carol continues to be my teacher and mentor. I work closely with her, assist in her teacher training, and run Integral Breath Therapy Training in Europe. I am deeply grateful for this work and this gift that she has shared with the world. And to my dear friend Yonat, who stepped in and connected me to this work, steering me gently back to life when I did not have my hand on the helm of my boat. I am humbled that life has opened up this beautiful path that I get to dance down. I hope you will join me.

I am also extremely grateful to Edmundo Santos, the most incredible teacher, with so much knowledge and generosity of his time, knowledge, and experience. I continue to work with Edmundo as coordinator and teacher on Poiesis, trauma-informed embodiment, and Expressive Arts. He has opened up a new way for me to approach my own work and showed me that even when working with the Shadow, in fact especially when, we encase it in love, in curiosity, it doesn't need to be scary. There is great beauty in this work, in this enriching combination of finding the treasure within, our own inner healer. I call this 'el carrer del Mitg" and for this, I am eternally grateful.

If you would like to find out more, you can find me at Surrender To The Breath www.surrendertothebreath.com for training, events, and workshops, and join our community on Instagram: @surrendertothebreath for current events in Barcelona and online.

For grief support check out *How's Your Mourning?* a free bi-monthly support group online: https://www.eventbrite.es/e/hows-your-mourning-tickets-641261539527

If I can do it, so can you. Happy breathing xx

Stéphanie Vloeberghs

Triggers And Treats

https://www.linkedin.com/in/stephanie-vloeberghs-1104a9114
https://www.facebook.com/113790351721413
https://www.instagram.com/triggersandtreats
www.triggersandtreats.com
https://cherrydeck.com/sukipollock

Stéphanie Vloeberghs is a multifaceted professional with a passion for enhancing well-being through her expertise in music, visual arts, and therapeutic practices. As a singer, photographer, and seasoned massage therapist, Stéphanie has honed her craft over 14 years. Her mastery of Relaxation Massage, Sports Massage, Reflexology (focusing on hands, feet, and head), and Trigger Point Therapy sets her apart in the field, with a particular emphasis on the long-term effectiveness of the latter.

Stéphanie's dedication to excellence extends beyond her practice; she also shares her knowledge and skills through teaching courses and workshops in Barcelona, Belgium, and Mallorca.

Her extensive clientele spans diverse demographics, including athletes, children, the elderly, pregnant women, and rehabilitation patients. Stéphanie's collaborative approach with medical professionals such as doctors, chiropractors, therapists, and surgeons underscores her commitment to comprehensive care and holistic healing. Her services extend across various settings, from clinics and healing centers to private residences and retirement homes.

Driven by a passion for understanding the human body, Stéphanie has immersed herself in study and hands-on experience, gaining profound insights into the interplay between lifestyle, behavior, and physical well-being. Through her work, she has observed recurring patterns and recognising the importance of empowerment through education, she advocates for broader awareness of the benefits of massage therapy and encourages individuals to learn the basic massage techniques for self-care and mutual support.

What Stéphanie endeavors to convey most clearly is the paramount interconnectedness of all facets within our bodies. It's all connected—body, blood circulation, nervous system, thoughts, our emotional realm, muscles, and all other bodily systems; one cannot function without the other, and each has a profound effect on the next.

She also offers online coaching sessions titled "The Best Life Blueprint," where she collaborates with you to examine your lifestyle comprehensively, addressing all necessary facets. Together, she crafts a holistic step-by-step plan, a "blueprint," tailored to your life, offering profound insights that enable you to perceive yourself with newfound clarity. With her guidance, cultivating the necessary discipline to integrate this new routine into your life becomes effortless.

Stéphanie's dedication to promoting well-being extends to her online platform, where she shares valuable insights on anatomy, psychology, and self-care through her instagram page, blog and website, www.triggersandtreats.com. Through her holistic approach and wealth of experience, Stéphanie endeavors to empower individuals to cultivate a deeper understanding of their bodies and harness the transformative power of touch for enhanced physical and emotional health.

TRIGGERS AND TREATS

By Stéphanie Vloeberghs

PREVIOUSLY

I was born in Antwerp, Belgium in 1983 with a serious back deformity which had, and will continue to have, a big impact on many facets and decisions in my life.

I have always been an athletic person. I played tennis and danced at a high level for eight years. These two sports were passions that I practiced every day but I had to quit them both as soon as I learned about my physical distortion. Out of fear of causing even greater damage to my body, I blocked everything out and retreated to my room.

That's when I discovered a new outlet in drawing, singing, and writing. Social contact had become difficult for me because I felt different than others and more sensitive. Vulnerable. Over the years I felt safer in the company of my own world.

That changed later once I turned 17 when my years of hermit life shifted into the need to seek the thrill again in the outside world. I felt like I had to share what I had been creating within the fantasy walls of my room over the past three years.

I started making a living as a professional singer and performed throughout Belgium and neighboring countries. I played at all the festivals, clubs, company parties, TV shows, and private parties among all classes. I performed with many professional musicians and various bands from my country.

But what I learned very quickly was that this is not an easy world to hold your fort strong as a young woman. Especially when you are mostly surrounded by men every day, who occasionally have other intentions or a different, less appropriate image of making music.

I have never once let myself be persuaded by sexist pressure, but for that, I had to pay a different price in return. If you had an opinion or indicated your boundaries, they lost interest in working with you in a professional manner, or they suddenly found your ideas no longer as spectacular as they did in the beginning.

That's how I moved from one project or job to another. It shook my confidence tremendously, especially not yet being aware at that age of what was actually going on. But I learned fast.

The entertainment industry is often a selfish world of appearances and ego, and as an oversensitive woman who ended up in that field, I was too young and naive to mentally hold my ground.

While I simply wanted to move others and express my feelings through my art, writing, my voice, and by playing together with true musicians, I was pulled from left to right by everyone who wanted to benefit from my talent. This was not necessarily always directly from bad intentions, but never once had anyone really asked me what I wanted.

They wanted to have control over me.

There was no interest in my inner world, only in how they could benefit from me. I was exploited. Everything was determined for me. If I ever dared to express my thoughts and feelings, my opinion was suppressed or I was exaggerating or being dramatic. My voice was silenced.

All that I had created for years meant nothing anymore. This weighed so heavily on me mentally and physically that I completely lost touch with myself. The world and all the dreams that I created and believed in had crumbled, and there was barely anything left.

When I wasn't performing, I partied until I numbed myself to the point that my whole body ached from morning to night on a daily basis, and I became very depressed. I no longer knew my own thoughts.

SHIFT

The moment that I realized that I stopped enjoying singing, I decided to leave everything behind and travel to a place where I could start from scratch. Where I could remember my own voice again. My heart. I wanted to give myself a chance to heal, and it was crucial that I did.

People told me I was running away but these were the same people who themselves lived in self-destruction on a daily basis. Addicted to cigarettes, alcohol, drugs, food, sex, or any alternative that makes people not face their own problems. That, for me, is the worst way to flee.

Yes, I was running, but in a way that gave me the space and opportunity to listen to myself again and shut down all the noise around me which had become unavoidable. So at that moment, the only way to actually heal was to leave. I bought a ticket without knowing when I was going to come back.

HEAL

I got introduced to the world of massage therapy in Puerto Viejo, a Caribbean village south of Costa Rica. This village was known for being the place where all musicians traveling to Costa Rica would pass by to jam together. So it was on my bucket list. I ended up living there for a year.

Learning to live with pain since my childhood has always been a challenge for me and one of the biggest reasons why I always found more peace in warm places. My body suffered less in the company of sun, nature, and seawater.

In Puerto Viejo, I had my daily morning walks on the beach with the five same street dogs walking alongside me. I went swimming every day. I learned how to surf, which was a very good boost for my confidence because I had to rely on the strength of my body again for balance. I ate nothing but fresh fruit and vegetables and drank coconut water with a straw straight from the nut. I was healing. I found my thoughts again. It wasn't easy, but I faced them.

That year in Costa Rica, I started writing my own music again, and after one month I performed on a weekly basis with truly kind musicians from all over the world by singing my own songs. Nobody knew who I was and I had the

space to just be me. During my spare time, I delved into the world of massage.

I became friends with a massage therapist who opened up my vision of the human body. She introduced me to trigger point therapy and during that year I also learned how to apply it myself. For the first time in 10 years, I was living pain-free.

CALLING

That's when and why I became a passionate massage therapist myself after that. I experienced firsthand the enormous benefits it has for the body and how it relieves pain. Ever since going to Costa Rica, I have been studying intensively about general, human well-being and I will never stop doing so.

The body, the muscles, and the link with organs and how everything in our system is also connected to emotional levels and vice versa is so interesting.

Trigger point therapy particularly helped me the most over the years, and I have helped many clients also get rid of their chronic physical and/or mental problems.

Professional ballet dancers, basketball players, car crash survivors, addicts, a child who suffered from anxiety, a mother who lost her son, a woman who had pain in her legs every evening since she was a child, someone who wanted to stop smoking, ... and so on.

AFTERLIFE

For a couple of months, my condition has started to affect my nervous system and this is not reversible. This will eventually lead to Parkinson's. I am already in the first phase of the disease, but I have it under control thanks to my self-knowledge about my body and the therapies that are capable of slowing down the entire process.

Swimming, meditation, no processed food, daily hikes, breathing exercises, yoga, massage therapy, ...

Unfortunately, I had to stop giving massages on a daily basis. However, I will continue to pass on all the knowledge I have gained through various alternative means.

It's too important not to share.

Without it, I would have been in much more pain these last few years, and I feel it is almost my human duty to do something with it for those who are struggling with chronic pain and are unaware of the benefits of massage therapy. I speak about all kinds of back problems, muscle diseases, nervous disorders, and more.

My new focus now is digging into the nervous system and especially the link and effect of emotional damage to our body and brain.

The biggest message that I want to make especially clear to as many people as possible is how *everything* in our body is connected, and how literally *every* decision and *everything* in our environment can impact our health.

Especially in these times.

MATTER THE FACTS

The gap between forty years ago and the current era is huge. An enormous evolution has taken place due to the rise of the internet and technological inventions that each appear with their monthly updates.

As someone from a generation where as teenagers we simply played outside in the garden in our spare time and giggled excitedly among our friends if a boy at the school gate so much as asked our name, I must admit that I am very overwhelmed by the absolute abundance of offers and advertisements nowadays and by the rise of social media where everything that used to belong safely to our private world is now openly displayed.

And it only seems to grow by the day. Each person or company competes with the other and looks for ways to make their product excel. For example, you almost have to go to college to possess the knowledge to be capable of separating the wheat from the chaff in food products. It's almost exhausting to keep up, but I have no choice; I owe it to myself. I want to be aware of what I eat, how what I buy is produced, and which company is behind it.

If a pair of pants is sewn by a child who is being exploited in a third-world country for the profit of a millionaire in order to become even richer, then I will not buy them. If a food product is full of added unnatural substances, processed to keep it "fresh" longer, then I won't buy it. We are unaware of the effect of these added substances on our overall health.

If we were to banish them from our daily lives, there would undoubtedly be far fewer cancer patients, patients with Crohn's disease, anxiety, depression, nervous diseases, and much more.

On my website, I wrote an article about processed food.

MYOFASCIAL PAIN SYNDROME

As a massage therapist, I have worked with athletes, children, the elderly, pregnant women, rehabilitation patients, addicts, the mentally disabled, psychiatric patients, and more. Often in close collaboration with doctors, chiropractors, therapists, and surgeons in clinics, healing centers, retirement homes, and people's homes.

I have built and maintained a personal bond with many clients, and it always gives me a lot of satisfaction to see how my therapies have made a positive impact in all their lives.

I have 14 years of experience in relaxation massage, sports massage, foot, hand, and head reflexology and I am specialized in trigger point

therapy. This is, in my opinion, the most efficient massage therapy in the long run for people who suffer from recurring blockages, painful muscle, or mental complaints for a long period of time.

After overstressing, injuries, or overuse, trigger points will inevitably arise and cause tension and pain throughout the whole muscle.

When this pain persists and progresses to a chronic state, doctors call it Myofascial Pain Syndrome.

Myofascial pain is a very common syndrome. Many people suffer from it a couple of times in their lifetime without even realizing it.

If you have myofascial pain syndrome, you feel pain and tenderness in muscles in a specific part or multiple parts of your body.

This pain and tenderness are usually related to multiple trigger points connected in a web around the painful area. The trigger points make communication more difficult within the network of the entire body system. That is why Trigger Point Therapy is a very effective treatment.

DIG DEEP

When I come across a blocked trigger point while I'm giving a massage, I work on it deeply. First, I gently massage the tissue around it in a constructive way towards the core to minimize the pain. When I finally address the source, I guide my clients in this last, most intense part of the process by making them breathe through it until they become one with the discomfort. And accept.

If they resist, their muscles will tense and I can't get through. If they accept the pressure of that trigger point, it will untangle and disappear more each time with every breath.

As goes life.

When we deny pain or ignore stressful situations and escape into numbing alternatives, it just piles up and hits us later, harder each time. If we deal with them, they are less likely to creep into our system to attach and escalate. Over time they will fade and disappear.

Our mind is completely connected to our body and the other way around. Shift your mental resistance into acceptance and it will physically let go of all that is attached to it.

GOLDEN TOOL

Massage therapy is a golden tool for stress reduction and pain relief. I have witnessed countless times with my own eyes that it's very beneficial regardless of what physical or mental ailments you have. It improves circulation, sleep quality, and flexibility, and decreases muscle stiffness and joint inflammation.

It helps with a quicker recovery in rehabilitation and between workouts and it strengthens our immune system. :SEP:

If it were up to me, everyone would get a massage once a month (per week is still too wishful thinking for now) reimbursed by the government. The world would look completely different.

I also teach basic massage techniques in Barcelona and Belgium because I want people to be able to apply this at home to their family or friends when they suffer from headaches, stress, or blockages before taking pills or heading straight to a doctor or physical therapist. In many cases, you can remove or prevent ailments yourself by applying these massage techniques.

AWARENESS

During my years as a massage therapist, I have noticed that far too many people are not aware of the state of their bodies.

Nor the importance of the connection between mind and body.

We have forgotten how our essential needs play a crucial role in our overall well-being. Many of us are not even aware of what these essential needs are. Or life's essence in general…

So many of us are falling asleep. We are not alive in this life. Not in the way we owe it to our soul.

The older we get, the harder it is to wake up again to our core or our calling. We become numb; we stop listening to our inner voice, to what our body is telling us, because of the daily distractions that make us completely lose sight of nature and our own.

"We are losing touch with touch".

LEARN FROM CHILDREN BY SHOWING THEM HOW

Children are still pure.

Kids are the future.

It is our responsibility to guide them in the right direction.

For me, that doesn't mean educating them in a direction that is determined by us. Everyone is different, everyone has their calling, and if we have it all figured out for them from the start, it becomes very hard for them to determine this for themselves.

They will start to feel limited without understanding why they are still in the hands of their parents, teachers, and the adult environment all around them at that age.

They don't realize that what we teach them becomes their second nature. That's why it's so important that we show them all the tools they have within themselves and their environment, at all times. We should remind them to stay true to their original nature. Teach them that they can feed their essential needs in a healthy way.

TREAT THE TRIGGERS

We are responsible for the environment children find themselves in, where they can be inspired and stimulated in a productive way. Where they learn to live consciously with themselves and all that surrounds them.

For example, if it were up to me, no cell phones would be allowed in schools. I would make daily meditation sessions mandatory from an early age to learn to deal with being overwhelmed by everything around us and what inevitably triggers us every hour, if not minutely.

From a young age, it should be conditioned into our entire system that when negative thoughts or worries consume us, we can immediately transform them into a state of mind that serves only productive purposes.

We must learn to be aware that we have all of this in our own hands. Meditation is a golden tool for this. Just like sports, massage, and nature.

All the daily, impactful events creep into our heads as well as our bodies. It's all connected. For example, If we are upset or scared about something, our heart rate increases, or we have more difficulty sleeping at night.

If our body doesn't get the rest it needs, some body systems may function less as required (digestive issues, low or high blood pressure, back or neck pain, etc.).

If we don't discharge these triggers on a daily basis, we create mental and physical blockages which lead to migraines, anxiety, tumors, depression, and so on.

Mind affects the body which affects the mind again.

Everyone should learn how to harvest their own food, not just for an hour a week in one trimester a year as a science project, but through all seasons. This is the only way I see how we can learn to understand the concept of nature again. Of essence. And if there is one thing that is more crucial now than ever, it is this.

We are completely losing sight of nature, as well as our own innate natures. We are losing touch with our core, with touch.

When we see people dancing and even hugging or kissing on the street, it has become like something we only see in movies. It shouldn't be something that makes some of us feel uncomfortable but instead something that is considered completely normal. It has become a more normal sight to see someone walking on the streets staring down at their phone than seeing a couple smiling and holding hands, or just a person walking, looking around, and taking his environment in.

Back to our core - we need to go back. We need to take a good, deep look again at where we come from, not only as humans in a historical evolutionary way, but from our own perspective.

To do that, we have to fight back by not giving in to all the noises around us, by digging deep, and by mattering the facts.

And most of all, by listening in the first place to our own voice.

SELF-LOVE AND FREEDOM

As John Lennon wrote, "As soon as you're born, they make you feel small, by giving you no time instead of it all."

That's why it is so important to take time for yourself. Every day.

To stay close to your soul, to listen to what your body is telling you.

If something feels off, it means there is something wrong. If you can't figure out the reason why? Explore... Listen to what your inner voice is trying to tell you, your intuition.

Close your eyes for a minute, breathe, and meditate. And before you do, ask for insight; it will come to you when you surrender to whatever state you're in. Give yourself the chance to heal.

In order to accept who you are, you need to know yourself and what makes you happy and what doesn't.

As I reflect on my journey of self-discovery and healing, I can't help but marvel at how exploring the depths of my back pain has brought me profound knowledge of human nature and its well-being.

I've never regretted anything in my life. Because in the end, I have always remained true to myself. It has not been an obstacle-free course, but this has taught me to indicate my boundaries, which is one of the greatest acts of self-love.

In this way, I have created an environment for myself that feels safe and surrounded by like-minded souls. Through diligent research, seeking expert advice, and embracing different therapies, I've not only alleviated the physical discomfort with my mind but also found a newfound sense of inner peace and resilience in music and writing.

My experiences have taught me that sometimes, the path to healing is a winding one, filled with unexpected twists and turns. Yet, it is through this exploration that I've not only mended my body as well as I can but also nurtured my soul, emerging stronger and more grateful for the precious gift of life and most of all for the person I am today.

And for me, there is no greater definition of pure happiness and freedom.

Lily Streames-Smith

Self-Love with Lily
Self-Love & Mindset Coach

https://www.facebook.com/profile.php?id=100087325299670
https://www.instagram.com/selflovewithlily

Lily Streames-Smith is a certified self-love and mindset coach who specialises in transforming women's lives through the power of self-love. In particular, she helps women to transmute their self-talk from criticism to compassion. She became a self-love coach following her own decade long battle with her mental health.

To learn more about Lily Streames-Smith and how she can help you to transform your life through self-love, visit @selflovewithlily on Instagram.

EMERGE WITH SELF-LOVE WITH LILY

By Lily Streames-Smith

Growing up is a wild ride, full of twists and turns. I don't think any of us come out of our teenage years completely unscathed. It's this crazy mix of trying to figure out who you are, what you enjoy and where you want to go in life, whilst being bombarded with messages of how you 'should' be from the outside world. Everyone's got their opinions and they can feel like they drown out your own thoughts or sometimes we even end up convincing ourselves that other people's hopes are our own dreams or preferences. There's this intense undercurrent of expectations placed on us all throughout life, but it feels particularly difficult to navigate as a teenager. There is the pressure to have your whole life planned out, to fit into societal norms, keep up with fashion trends, excel in extra-curricular activities, the list is endless. I am also part of the generation muddling through these struggles during the birth of social media. Not only was I trying to find my place in the microcosm of my life but I now also had access to polished and idealised images of life from all around the world.

It felt like a maze of challenges that came without a map, guidebook, or instructions. I was lost. The self-talk in my brain was one of deep criticism and self-hatred, leaving me desperately seeking from external sources, the approval and validation I so deeply lacked within. My reality began to reinforce my subconscious belief that I was not enough. I thought if I could match society's ideal, if I had the perfect grades, body, and boyfriend I would find happiness and contentment. The little girl inside me would finally feel worthy. That the voice in my head would magically morph from my harshest critic to a celebratory cheerleader. However, in my pursuit of these goals, I would not achieve the happiness and fulfilment I was aiming for but instead I would fall into a 10-year battle with depression, anxiety, and an eating disorder.

Little did I realise that it was this desperate need to be perfect and control my external world that was actually the fuel for my depression rather than the antidote to it. My story is proof that self-love and your commitment to it is the only control and discipline you need. This is a story of hope and also a reminder of the power we all hold within ourselves.

If we rewind to my childhood, you'll find an energetic and carefree child, totally unfazed about her appearance, body, or caloric intake. This is where most of us begin, but few of us remain. It's a well-known fact that the early chapters of our life are crucial in forming behaviours, responses and belief systems that shape who we become and how we show up in later life. A part of our mind, the subconscious, absorbs all the messaging we receive as a child, the good, the bad and the ugly. This then becomes the software our brain runs on. It might sound strange, but considering the subconscious governs a whopping 95% of our daily actions, the messaging we receive growing up is truly impactful. It wasn't one traumatic event for me that ignited my mental health battles, it was a whole mixture of different voices and behaviours that surrounded me. My mum worked at the local health club for the majority of my childhood, so I spent many hours there surrounded by self-deprecative conversations about bodies and food intake. Not just that, I also received an influx of compliments on my naturally petite frame. Although harmless, I quickly felt pressure to maintain this body, as it provided so much validation having a body that other people deeply desired. Puberty had other plans, so naturally my body changed, and I gained a little weight. Although, it was nothing drastic, the compliments I was receiving seemed to dry up and sadly, that left me questioning my worth more than ever. If I wasn't slim, who was I? What was I good at?

The next culprit that came into play was social media, inundating me with unrealistic body standards, gruelling workouts, and diets only capable of fuelling a 2-year-old. This encouraged the relentless criticism already present in my mind. The content further convincing me I wasn't pretty or thin enough and that I needed to work harder to be that. This fixation on the external, on the contours of my body, drained me mentally and physically. I didn't go to social events anymore and if I did, I was barely even present. Physically yes, mentally I was entirely somewhere else. Each day brought anxiety and scrutiny over every dietary and movement choice. I felt so isolated, like every other woman effortlessly had a gorgeous physique and somehow a healthy relationship with food too. That felt a million miles away from my experience, desperately trying to manipulate my body to be 'perfect' trapping myself in a cycle of bingeing, restricting and overexercising. I was chasing this dream body with the belief it would bring happiness and success, but it simply made me miserable, isolated, and anxious.

Don't get me wrong, it wasn't only the messages I was receiving from my environment that played into my battles with food, exercise, and my body. It was also a remedy for the emotional rollercoaster that comes with adolescence, a way of pushing away the uncomfortable emotions that I had no clue how to deal with. The feelings of not being good enough, desirable enough, academic enough, beautiful enough, skinny enough. You name it. At the time, I genuinely believed that losing weight and having abs would fix everything in my life, like some miraculous cure, and at age 16 I thought I'd found the perfect solution to this all. I would follow my dreams of going to a performing arts school to train as a professional dancer. Surely, this would be the key to happiness, attractiveness, and success? I would lose weight as I was dancing for hours and hours each day. I would be an even more talented performer. I would finally have a clear identity, know who I was and feel worthy.

As you can imagine, my dreams of what this performing arts school would provide were quickly met with a totally different reality. A reality that deepened the echoes of inadequacy inside me. I was surrounded by so many incredible dancers, all of which I felt were more talented, slimmer, and confident than me. This raised my already unrealistic expectations of myself and left me feeling completely out of my depth. I attempted to lose weight as a quick fix, but I would eventually binge when the emotions got too unbearable. This cycle became more intense and intolerable over time, so I had to make the tough call to ditch my dream and focus on my mental health. Leaving I felt like a complete failure, but now I look back and can clearly see I was anything but. That decision took courage and was one of the first times where I truly chose myself, where I began to embark on my journey with self-love. I knew I couldn't tackle this alone anymore; it was finally time to seek professional help.

I still remember making the doctor's appointment to finally tell someone about my mental health struggles. It had been my secret for three whole years, and I was so nervous of the reception I'd receive. Would the doctor believe me? Would I be classed as 'sick' enough to get help? Would they have to tell my family? Only looking back now can I see how riddled I was with shame surrounding my eating disorder and mental health but opening up about my struggles brought a huge sense of relief. Finally telling someone what it was like in my mind and them listening and offering to get me support, I felt hope that things could change. The doctor referred me to the child and adolescent mental health services (CAMHS), where I received cognitive behavioural therapy to help shed some of the layers of unhealthy behaviours, restrictive rules and relentless inner criticism that were holding me captive. It put me on the road to recovery, I was feeling happier and able to live life a little more like your average teenager.

These newfound feelings of happiness made me realise I wanted to help others with their mental health journeys too. At this point, I made the decision to study a Psychology degree to learn exactly how. University life threw new challenges at me though. The freedom that others relished in, was a field day for the perfectionist in me. I felt all the pressures to utilise the newfound freedom, ace my academics and create lifelong friendships, whilst also trying to get to grips with adult responsibilities like cooking, cleaning, and washing. It felt so overwhelming that I even considered dropping out of university all together but luckily, I was met with so much support that persuaded me to stay. Each week I worked with a mentor to question my perfectionist thoughts, express my feelings, and start recognising the self-care practices that calmed me during tricky times. You'd think adding a part-time job to my list would send me over the edge but actually it did quite the opposite. It made me realise that once you're in the working world, your grades really aren't that significant. That there are so many successful people in this world, without degrees, A-Levels and GCSEs so yes, it's good to try your best but it's also important to remember they won't dictate the rest of your life. This realisation helped me to find a better work-life balance, I prioritised managing my mental health rather than sacrificing it all just for some numbers on a piece of paper.

Graduation was one of my proudest life moments and after the high of it, I just wasn't ready to go straight into a full-time job. Instead, I decided to travel some of the world hoping this incredible experience would leave me feeling completely carefree, happy, and present in the moment. Surprisingly, although I gained physical freedom, I was still grappling with the loud inner critic in my mind. Throughout my travels, I never fully allowed myself to embrace each new place and cuisine as I was constantly in my own thoughts trying to achieve the perfect bikini body. I look back now and feel sad for that version of myself, the version that felt my body needed to look a certain way to enjoy life and would miss out on life's pleasures in the pursuit of that. After a few months, it was time to return home and get back to the real world.

Naively, I convinced myself the next change in environment would miraculously cure the negative and controlling thoughts in my mind. That a 9-5 job would be the solution. I'd be so busy all day that I'd have little time to think about what I was eating or how much exercise I was doing. Oh, how wrong I was. The job, while momentarily provided me with a sense of identity and validation, it wasn't long until the perfectionist in me grew louder again. It was at this moment, I realised that no matter the environment I found myself in, I continually fell into the same, unhealthy thought patterns and behaviours. I was seeking external validation, I was trying to be liked by everyone, trying to be 'perfect.' The problem with that, is that perfection doesn't exist and my attempts to reach it were the very cause of my unhappiness. It was like a light switch flipped and I suddenly realised the only way to truly be happy was to turn inwards and listen to what was going on in my mind and body. Something I had been desperately avoiding for so long. I needed to listen to what I needed and wanted in each moment, not what others needed and wanted from me. I needed to put myself first and drown out the noise of expectations around me. I see now that the thoughts about food, exercise and my body were all protection strategies, they were ways I was trying to stay 'safe,' and 'in control.'

As I continued to look inward, I also started to explore compassion focused therapy, putting together the pieces surrounding my childhood and how they had influenced my thoughts and protective strategies as an adult. I reconnected to my strengths, values and what brought me joy in life. I learnt self-soothing strategies so I could regulate my emotions without always relying on others. It was at this point that inner child healing also came into my life. The inner child is the part of our subconscious mind that contains everything we learnt as a child about emotions, safety, how to form connections and who we are in the world. Connecting with this part of myself allowed me to understand my behaviours, triggers, wants, and needs. Just picturing a little girl inside of me instantly shifted something inside of me. When critical thoughts came up I no longer chose to believe them, instead I started to stand up for myself and shift them to more compassionate ones. I no longer felt like a victim, I felt empowered knowing I could give myself everything I needed. It was this shift in my internal world that completely transformed everything externally too.

I finally began offering myself the same care, love, and compassion that I had so generously given to others my whole life. I let go of friendships and relationships where I didn't feel safe, loved, and supported. In turn, beautiful, more aligned ones showed up. I stopped being constantly ill and tired because I started to slow down and give my nervous system the rest it so deeply required. I began soothing the negative thoughts and feelings that arose by comforting my inner child as opposed to just stuffing them down with food. I no longer wanted to criticise myself in the mirror anymore knowing that a little version of me was always listening. I let go of the desire to be super skinny knowing that that body represented suffering and not truly living. My new curvier body instead, reflected a life full of adventures, joy and contentment. I chose to do movement for enjoyment rather than purely to burn calories. I traded the rush that society imposes on us for self-care time each morning and night. My wardrobe became a form of self-expression, not a tool for approval or a means to 'flatter' my figure. I felt grateful for the simple things and could finally see the magic in life. The beauty in myself, inside and out. I realised I never needed the perfect body, job, or boyfriend, what I needed was a different mindset. I needed self-love.

And that is why I am where I am today. A self-love coach helping women to break free from their inner critic, self-doubt, and societal expectations so they can step into their most calm, confident, and fulfilled self. We all deserve to experience true happiness, peace, and success. The key to which is self-love. So, wherever you are on your own journey, I do hope you'll come and join my community on Instagram @selflovewithlily. Get ready to start feeling more empowered, confident, and able to navigate your internal world.

For now, I'll leave you with this. True happiness isn't a prize awarded by anything or anyone outside of you; it's an inside job.

Do not miss my freebie where you can learn more about the mind and body connection even if you are just starting out! It is a great resource for anyone.

Love,
Paula Echeverri

www.ingramcontent.com/pod-product-compliance
Lightning Source LLC
Chambersburg PA
CBHW071005120626
46546CB00003B/944